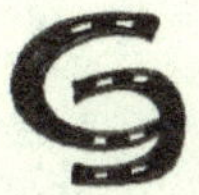

I0836021

Walking Around

With

Fante and Bukowski

and other essays

art, sex, politics and the ups and downs of cultural displacement

Patricio Maya

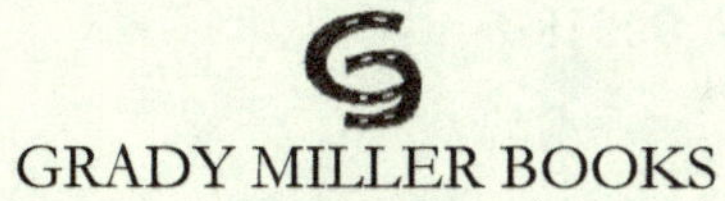

Walking Around with Fante and Bukowski and other essays

Author's photo by Carlos Serrano

Cover design by Nick Chung
(vividcolorprinting.com)

ISBN: 978-0986273407

Manufactured in the United States of America.

Editor: Grady Miller

Please contact the publisher at:
gradymillerbooks@gmail.com

1236 1/8 N. Cahuenga Blvd.
Hollywood, CA 90038

For Chloe Dietkus

—in Bramble, by the creek

Contents

PART TWO: POLITICS

PART THREE: SELF

Introduction: *On Wandering Off and Finding Your Way Back*

I was run over by a car in Quito, Ecuador, when I was 4 years old.

My elders would always warn me against wandering off because, for instance, the gypsies could kidnap you, take you to Colombia or Peru and force you to work in a circus for the rest of your life. Or you could end up injured under a car. My nanny, Margarita, whom I loved as a second mother, had also been warned. Whenever we went for a walk, she would make sure to grasp my hand. Her job depended on it. But for some reason I was set on fleeing at the slightest distraction. The day it happened Margarita and I were crossing a busy intersection (back then in Quito pedestrians never waited for red lights). I don't remember much. Somehow I managed to let go and I think it was a white pickup truck. I have a sense of the commotion and the hospital and the relief after the doctors confirmed I was unscraped. People said it was a miracle. Still, I'm sure Margarita was chastised. Wherever you are now, dear

Margarita, I would like to take this opportunity to apologize to you. It was my own fault.

But I couldn't help it. Wandering off was in my blood. I even got lost abroad once. During my first grade summer break, Grandmother Carmen took all of us grandchildren to Florida for the summer. We went to Disneyworld, the Tampa aquarium, chewed on rolls of pink Bubble Tape, bought neon-colored backpacks with big clocks on the back, and listened to Milli Vanilli and Gloria Estefan ad nauseam. This was my first encounter with the United States. I've gone over it countless times in my head. Someday I'd like to write about it, but it would have to come out as fiction because time has begun erasing those memories. During the Florida trip I again wandered off as soon as I could. It happened at a kind of flea market near Miami. I remember being amazed at all the pink-skinned grown-ups speaking that strange nasal language known as English. (The U.S.A. was like a dream then; now Ecuador, the old country, seems like a dream to me). My father eventually found me. Or maybe I found my way back on my own. I can't remember. It's been so long.

I would always find my way back. That much I know. Though there were times when I would truly get lost. I particularly remember one time in the fifth grade when Omar Orbe, Francisco Martinez and I (all of us wearing cardigans and skinny blue ties) ran into a bull and its angry Quechua-speaking owner while exploring the Quito countryside. Or as grownups would put it: "trespassing into someone else's hacienda." The old woman tried to whack us with a broom, but we ducked down and scurried away. We were pros at that. And loved it. Real fear! Real danger! Real wrongdoing! Those kinds of adventures could morph into myths within minutes. Hundreds of future conversations could be fueled by them.

This restlessness to wander off is intimately linked to being a writer. I think most writers have it. But in my case, it precedes my falling in love with writing when I was 15 at Hollywood High School. My desire to get lost in other worlds is more primal than my desire to create, but I don't know much about psychology and won't get into that. I do, however, have a sort of method. After years and years of practice, I have realized that for me there are only two ways of wandering off, though they might be the same way: 1) playing detective, 2) pretending you are lost until it really happens.

But I should clarify something before going on. I have never ever wandered off wishing to stay lost. Wandering off not intending to find your way back is not getting lost at all. That's called running away. In order to really get lost you must have the desire to come back home. I have never wanted to run away from home. I have strayed pretty far by way of books, traveling or even pretense, but I have always wanted to return to my original affections, culture, faith, language and values. I have not always managed to go back, many times for the better, but I have tried.

The reward behind wandering off lies in coming back. Once you're back, you see things differently. And then you can start writing. Wordsworth kind of knew what he was talking about with his "emotion recollected in tranquility" stuff. Let me put it another way: What good does it do you to get kidnapped by gypsies at age 5 and learn how to tame wild lions if you can't come back home ten years later to show off your new skills to your parents and friends?

Not that I've ever been kidnapped. And I couldn't even tame Rusty, the senile orange cat I lived with for years, let alone wild lions. But I have taken some voyages. I was brought to the United States in 1995, right before my teenage years started. There weren't any bull-owning Quechua-speaking women to get kicks from in Los Angeles, but there were plenty of worlds to get into (trespass as it were). Not long after arriving from Quito, for instance, I befriended and spent countless hours with a Russian-speaking, ethnically Armenian girl born in Azerbaijan who had a pierced septum, green hair, and was obsessed with Kurt Cobain even more than I was. Diana and I were best friends for years. We came of age as culturally displaced, Americanized, "alternative" Hollywood High kids together. All those punk rock shows and lazy afternoons watching indie movies like *Ghost World* and *Donnie Darko* with her bewildered mom, Rima, were such a blast. Ah, Rima's borsch was such a revelation to my Andean palate.

In high school, I got into books, thought I was a Buddhist, an anarchist, a vegetarian, and, at the beginning of college, a Morrissey-influenced aesthete. Since I lived in the States with an expired visa for years, I joined the political struggle of many other Hispanic immigrants who'd had it much harder in their home countries than I had in mine. In college, I fell in love with a girl from San Francisco, drove with her from coast to coast twice, read Joan Didion and Susan Sontag and Deborah Eisenberg, went to the Toronto Film Festival, lived in the Onondaga snow for a year, started critiquing photos, acquired too much student debt and finally moved to Sonoma County to live in a cabin by some blueberry bushes and an apple tree. I have worked as a pizza delivery guy, a theater critic, a vitamin salesman, a tennis coach, and an ESL teacher. I have not been the most goal-oriented guy in the world. But I have, as William Saroyan said in his life-changing intro to "The Daring Young Man in the Flying Trapeze," learned to breathe deeply, really tasted food when eating, slept well often, laughed like hell when I laughed, and got good angry when angry.

Even when many of the experiences above are not directly fleshed out in these essays —other collections will hopefully take care of that— with this intro I hope to state where I come from and why I have written about these particular subjects. Thank you for reading.

—Patricio Maya
Los Angeles, California

ART

Walking Around with Fante and Bukowski

Like other victims of the Hollywood dream, Arturo Bandini from Denver finds himself in a dive in Los Angeles, mulling over what to do with his life. He probably puts away one or two drinks, immersed in his two obsessions: elusive literary fame and the love of Camilla López, a defiant Mexican waitress. An older woman spies on Bandini from some corner. She has been able to decipher his turbulent inner life by virtue of observation.

Night falls. As usual, Bandini's dreary room on Bunker Hill has no amenities, no heat and no rest. There is a sheet of paper with randomly written sentences in his typewriter. Camilla dominates his thoughts like a whirlpool. At that moment the mysterious woman from the bar enters. She is older, she is Jewish, she has very black hair, and she has drunk herself to bravery.

They beat around the bush. Basically, the woman and Bandini exchange recaps of their lives and aspirations. She wants to seduce him. He is indecisive. On one hand, there is the eroticism of the night, and on the other, the decadence glimpsed through the woman's boozy breath. He wants to kick her out or have her. But no. He lets her speak. She confesses about the spying, tells him about her husband who left her, and she recites a poem for him. She even shows him her horrible secret: her maimed loins.

She cries; he plays with her hair.

Meanwhile, a truce is established. She will go, but before going, she predicts that sooner or later Bandini will go to look for her. Bandini stays in his room with a name and an address scribbled on a piece of paper. The name is Vera Rivken. The address is in Long Beach, 22 miles away.

**

Ask the Dust is the most famous novel by John Fante, a seminal author in California literature. But the novel was forgotten until Charles Bukowski chanced on it in the late '70s in a public library and recommended it to an editor at Black Sparrow. The Black Sparrow Press edition appeared in 1980. Some 40 years had gone by since the nearly ignored first edition. Bukowski himself wrote the preface. This magnificent preface (as good as the one Juan Carlos Onetti wrote for Roberto Arlt in *Mad Toy*) opened John Fante's door wide to innumerable readers. It was a resounding success. Nowadays *Ask the Dust* is an essential novel of the so-called dirty realism of Los Angeles.

I first read Bukowski's preface around 2002, when I was 19 years old and I was studying at Los Angeles City College, the same community college where Bukowski, one of my literary gurus, had studied. During this period I spent a lot of time in a gigantic store that sold

CDs and books on the Sunset Strip, rereading poems from *War All the Time* by Bukowski before going to the movies or catching a punk rock concert.

Bukowski, the cursed poet of Los Angeles, wasn't big on deifying his literary forebears, but in that preface he manned up: "Fante was my god," he said.

Naturally I had to devour *Ask the Dust.*

And Bukowski was right. In Bandini, Fante captures a very particular mix of purity and ambition: that of the young writer. The descriptions of streets, corners, neighborhoods, and buildings stand out too. Everything is authentic. One goes out on the street after reading a novel by Fante, and the buildings emerge renewed. A mystique impregnates the streets. All the more if you are 19 years old, and you believe you're a poet and are willing to get lost in this tenuous dimension between books and reality. You walk downtown or on Wilshire, half stoned, asking yourself if here was where Nathanael West ate, if there was where William Saroyan brawled, if Bandini slept here, if Bukowski drank there. It is a kind of derangement. But there are worse ways to spend time when you are 19 years old.

Bukowski had also been possessed by the Fante mystique.

"Almost every day I walked by and I thought," he wrote in the preface, "is that the window Camilla crawled through? And, is that the hotel door? Is that the lobby? I never knew."

He didn't know because Bukowski had a rule: "I knew that the gods should be left alone, one didn't bang at their door."

**

When he finds himself dominated by Camilla López —he loves her; she doesn't love him— Bandini gets inspired by Casanova and Cellini, renowned Don Juans, possessing the same Italian blood as he. Bandini wants this force. He convinces himself that fornicating with Vera will grant the miracle that will enable him to seduce Camilla.

That's Bandini—erratic, impulsive.

"Let the conquering spirit possess you," he tells himself and heads down Bunker Hill to the Red Line station.

**

I leave my apartment in Little Tokyo. The building where I live is located right before the bridge that connects downtown to East Los Angeles; that is, on the opposite side of Bunker Hill, which still exists. The sky is cloudless. I calculate that the temperature will be around 73 degrees. It is a perfect spring day in Los Angeles.

A little more than a decade has elapsed since I first read Bukowski's preface. Now less susceptible to literary mystiques, I have decided to experience again a minor part of *Ask the Dust*: the handful of pages where Bandini takes the 22 mile trip from Bunker Hill to Long Beach, in search of Vera Rivken, the dark woman from the bar.

On his trip Bandini sought eroticism. I seek signs of the 1930s.

Why?

Maybe an exercise in nostalgia or a way of restoring my already tired relationship with the city I grew up in.

There are worse ways to spend time when you are 30

years old.

I crossed the small Japanese neighborhood from east to west. There aren't many old buildings. The people are the same as ever. Reaching Main Street, the Civic Center opens up with its imposing governmental constructions. On 4th Street can be seen turn-of-century buildings like the Barclay Hotel and Farmers & Merchants Bank. No time to go inside. Bandini surely didn't stop anyplace. I take a couple of pictures on my iPhone and walk on.

I go by a place that looks dangerous. White middle-class young people (and all that this implies) have arrived in downtown Los Angeles in recent years, but there still remain poor blocks that are predominantly African-American and Latino. I reach Main and 6th, where there was once a trolley station. The station no longer exists, but the building should. I find it next to Artisan House, a restaurant where an entrée costs $25. The old station is no longer even a public building. Now it's a luxury apartment house called the Pacific Electric Building.

Why does it bother me that Los Angeles is not like it used to be? Why am I bothered by gentrification, of which, to a certain degree, I am part of? I don't know. It doesn't matter.

A sullen security guard lets me enter the lobby. It is clean, well-cared for and has not been modified a great deal. There is a lot of light. But now it's just lofts! I wonder if I'm making myself clear: there are only a couple of photographs and a pair of plastic replicas behind glass acknowledging the old train station.

What did I expect? To find Camilla López serving coffee in the part adjacent to the lobby? To be able to speak with Bandini?

I walk on.

Eventually I pass by Pershing Square, a park right in the very middle of the city. A filthy old woman with a sick face and white hair asks me for change. I give it to her. She has beautiful blue eyes. There is something in her, in her stench, in her madness, and in her words, "God bless you, Happy Easter," that is more eternal than any building could ever be.

**

An attractive blonde is paying for her fare at a machine next to me. We exchange glances.

"The train is about to leave," she says to me, as we walk toward the station's lower platform.

I feel she is smiling. We quickly descend the stairs and board the train. She sits opposite me. The train leaves the station and rolls onto an elevated track.

The Metro Blue Line was built in 1990. It is the oldest and most congested in the Los Angeles subway system. The old Red Line trolleys that Bandini took closed in 1961. Lucky for me, the Blue Line retraces parts of the old Red Line. In other words, there are certain moments when I will behold the same landscapes that Bandini once beheld. To me, romantic dog that I am, that kind of stuff means something.

And yet, during the trip I think little about Bandini, little about Fante or even the blonde. I try to get settled. South Central, Watts, Willowbrook and Compton flit by. Many old houses and used car lots are visible. Mostly minorities. These places are the flipside of wealthy, white, organized and spotless Beverly Hills, West Los Angeles and Santa Monica. The truth is obvious. Los Angeles is a loosely segregated city.

**

A 40-something black man sits down beside me. His name is Ryan. He has a graying goatee, baggy pants, and gold earrings with the letters C and M in the left ear. He tells me that he is going home after work. He's tired. Seems like a good guy. Smiles a lot.

He says that he once saw a train hit a pedestrian.

"It knocked him down but it didn't run over him," he says. "If you can't even realize there's a huge train coming, it's your fucking fault."

I've seen this kind of rigor before.

**

A plump Mexican woman sits to my right. Her son, a charming, unkempt child of around 5 years old, sits to my left. A girl of around 9 sits in front. A taciturn man of around 40, presumably the father, stays standing. The woman and the boy keep passing a big plastic cup of soda back and forth over me. In fact, the child is almost sitting on my legs. The cup is sticky and the child truly unclean, but this does not bother me. The child has a cute face and has a right to be unbound by normal manners. What surprises me is that the woman, who speaks to her children in Spanish, does not excuse herself—neither verbally, nor even with a glance or body language. There is a kind of animosity in her movements. As if to exacerbate the situation, she orders her daughter, who is quite tall, to sit on her lap. I repeat: not even a simple *perdón* escapes her lips. All this contrasts greatly with the sweetness with which she caresses her daughter's hair, face and ears as she asks the girl countless loving questions: "How did it go in school today, *mi amor*? Are you okay? Did you like the food?"

**

The old houses and used car lots slip behind. The sky on the outskirts of Long Beach widens. Myriad conversations and pounding R&B spill through the train car.

I attempt to talk to a woman in a cute little wool cap and big gold hoops in her ears. Her name is Shannon, and she is chewing gum.

She confronts me first.

"You shouldn't have given money to that woman."

A while before a woman, a girl really, had crossed the train asking for "donations" for a baby tied to her chest. I gave her a dollar.

"I gave her money for the baby," I tell Shannon, failing to add that I felt guilty because I had already ignored various beggars.

"It's just an excuse to get your sympathy," she says, chewing gum.

There it is again—that rigor.

Rigor, not cruelty; cruelty has a different smell, a different color. These are rough neighborhoods. It is the toughness of a barnacle.

We arrive in Long Beach at 3:30 p.m. Before disembarking from the train, I shoot a glance toward where the attractive blonde was seated, but she is no longer there.

**

In *Ask the Dust*, Arturo Bandini says that Vera Rivken lived on the Long Beach Pike, an amusement park near the ocean.

I go to the pier. Until now Bandini's descriptions have proven more reliable than a GPS. This is how Fante describes Vera's apartment house: "It was down on the Long Beach Pike, across the street from the Ferris wheel and the Roller coaster. Downstairs a pool hall, upstairs a few single apartments. No mistaking that flight of stairs; it possessed her odor."

The first thing I see is a big sign that says "The Pike." The whole thing is a suburban-style shopping center; an ample parking lot with cheap buildings, painted loud colors, in which cars take precedence over humans. Places like Subway and McDonald's abound. Publicity pennants with photos of old Long Beach hang from the light poles. The photos might or might not be Photoshop recreations. My outsize skepticism tells me they are.

I keep walking toward the ocean looking and, in a way, sniffing for the apartments with that Vera Rivken odor Fante wrote about. The space in the amusement park is minimal. Not a lot of people there. I find a Ferris wheel. It is small, white and modern, as if it were portable. Suddenly, I see something. To my right there is an old-fashioned carousel. I almost run to it.

The person in charge, a teenage girl wearing thick glasses, brings me down from my cloud.

"It's not from here. It was brought in from somewhere else," she says. "You're a big fan of merry-go-rounds?"

"I'm looking for an apartment house. It's a very old building. It should be in front of a Ferris wheel."

"Speak to the guy who runs the train. He knows a lot

about history," she says, gesturing behind me.

What a beauty of an old train. Four little golf carts (on wheels!) linked together by chains and painted bright colors for the coming summer.

**

On the other side, where according to my calculations Vera Rivken's apartment house should be, there is a small pier with restaurants, boats, and stores. I cross the street. A little girl, tied to rubber cords, bounces on a trampoline. There is music and people smiling and taking pictures. The sweet cacophony of the people having fun by the Pacific on this Saturday afternoon preserves something of what Bandini's Long Beach must have been like in 1930.

In the information kiosk in front of the water stands an old man named Charles. I make a final attempt.

"Excuse me, sir, have you heard about the old Red Line to Long Beach?"

"Yes."

On the last attempt. That's how things go.

"When was the earliest time that you rode the Red Line?"

"In the 1930s, when I was in high school."

"You personally took the old train from the downtown station?"

"Yeah, a lot of times." He squints his eyes. "It looked like the train today. There were less buildings."

"The amusement park was the same as now and in the same place? Sorry about all these questions."

"Let me explain it this way, son. In the '30s if you wanted to come to where we are standing now, you would have had to be a good swimmer. The old amusement park was several blocks back. The old pier was filled in to construct the new pedestrian walkway. Do you understand what I'm saying?"

I do. So when Bandini was gazing at the dusk in 1930, he was looking in our direction, where we are now. In some way we're standing on the sea.

**

After possessing Vera Rivken, Bandini takes a nap. When he awakes, he takes advantage of Vera's absence to leave a couple of dollars on the table as a gesture of appreciation, "anxious to go and never come back."

He breathes deeply, feeling macho, invigorated and free of the oppressive control of Camilla, whom he loves and despises at the same time. He passes the Ferris wheel, the stores and the rest. He stops at a kiosk. He asks for a coffee.

But something isn't right.

It hits him suddenly, "like crashing or thunder, like death and destruction."

It is complete solitude. He walks by the pier quickly with the certainty that death is in his bones—not only his own death, but also Vera's, Camilla's, and the deaths of all the people on the pier. He feels the futility of life.

And guilt. "Mea culpa, mea culpa, mea maxima culpa," he repeats to himself.

Although he has read Nietzsche and Voltaire, Arturo Bandini knows that deep down, he is a profoundly Catholic man. He feels and knows —with unbelievable innocence— that by having fornicated with Vera he has committed a mortal sin.

Absorbed in the idea of his sin, he treads over the sand, gazes at the setting sun. When he stops and begins to shake sand out of his shoes, there's an earthquake.

In the distance, buildings heave. Bandini turns on his heel, runs toward the sea and then in the opposite direction, witnessing the shouts, turmoil, and all the dust.

"You did it, Arturo. This is the wrath of God. You did it."

**

I walk up and down the boards of the pier. I look at small boats, floating restaurants, floating funeral chapels, a lighthouse for sailors. The restaurants are packed. They serve fish tacos, french fries, spaghetti: the typical expensive menu, the typical lack of imagination. I go into Boston Restaurant, a chain like a thousand others. I sit at the counter and order three sliders and a Sprite. Three flat-screen TVs show college basketball, baseball, and the NBA. The music, if it can be termed that, is blasting. I eat slowly, so that when I leave, I can dwell in the dusk like Bandini does in the novel. As I eat, I think of the utter waste of time and money my literary penchants really are.

What if an earthquake broke in at this very moment?

I would kneel in a gesture of adoration. Such a coincidence between reality and literature would signify the existence of a supreme author. But there's no reassuring earthquake. I don't kneel, I don't jump, I don't cry, none of that. I pay, cross the street, go up the stairs and stop on a bridge made of white tubes. The sun seems to be coming down. I start reading the paragraph where Fante talks about the dusk: "It was the full ripeness of the evening, with the sun a defiant red ball as it sank beyond the sea." But it's not working. In my eagerness to leave, I have miscalculated the sunset. The sun here will probably not set for another twenty minutes. I put the tattered copy of *Ask the Dust* in my back pocket, unwilling to wait.

On the return train, Bukowski comes back to me from the preface like a mocking ghost: "The gods should be left alone, one doesn't bang at their door."

Translated from the Spanish by Grady Miller

Pedro Meyer's "The Breakfast"

Sometimes all you need to do is see a photo once and it stays with you for years. It becomes part of your mental archive, as it were. This photo by Mexican photographer Pedro Meyer made its way into my memory at once. I remember exactly where I saw it for the first time: BOMB Magazine, something like 10 years ago, maybe more. I didn't register the title or the photographer's name when I first saw it. All I know is that I kept the magazine and would go back to it once in a while just to look at the photo. I must have been like 19 or 20 and this is a beautiful shot, but I don't think my infatuation with it had to do with its formal achievement. It had to do with sexuality, independence, the messy room, her voluptuous body, and that mixture of wealth and abandon you can gather from the objects such as the thick rug, the white plates and that little night table on the left.

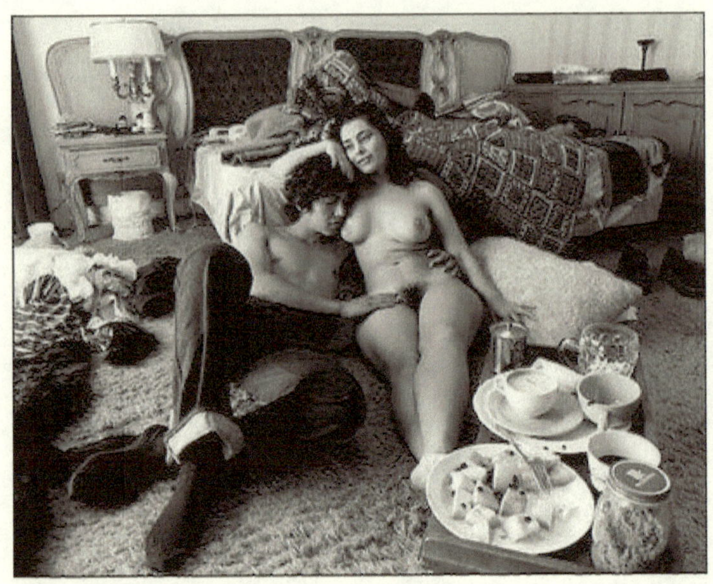

Pedro Meyer. "The Breakfast." 1975.

I could project all my teenage desires on it; so in a sense it was better that I didn't know much about Meyer. All I knew was that one day I would be with a woman with similar breasts and thighs, a woman who would not be afraid in the least to pose naked showing her pubic hair. She would be older than me, of course, and we would smoke pot and drink wine until really late and then we would wake up at noon and have a huge breakfast, after which we would proceed to have sex for the 4th time. She would be an artist like me and we would be always on the move from France to Spain to Morocco, always writing terribly sad poems and organizing some type of anarchist movement that would set ablaze the crumbling world order.

Why Do Hipsters Grow Mullets?

Time Magazine's LightBox blog was one of the first publications to cover Steven Rubin's drkrm show, "Vacationland." Some of the blog's readers, apparently Mainers, showed concern about the image of rural Maine put forth by Rubin's photos. They thought he made rural Maine look like "a shithole."

Here are four of the strongest reactions:

"Good Lord, way to give Maine a black eye."

"So these photos will be posted in LA where hipsters and elitists can mock Mainers? Are there any plans to bring these to Maine?"

"These photographs, while beautiful, depict rural Maine as being full of hopelessness."

"I grew up in Somerset County, graduating high school in 1982, when some of these photos were taken. Yes, these are beautiful 'raw' images of the subjects. But this is only a representation of one family and one sector of the region. Please don't think that all of central Maine is this desolate. We have beautiful spots too..."

Nobody wants his hometown depicted as some type of wasteland. That's understandable. The thing is, comments like the ones above miss a huge part of what "Vacationland" is about. Sure, the poor, "trashy," rural elements are all in the images. And they are important. They capture the everyday reality of some people who live under certain conditions and are part of a certain subculture. These people are not from Beverly Hills or downtown Los Angeles. But that's not, by far, the main part of the photo collection. In a sense, "Vacationland" has little to do with Elvis posters, junkyards and shotguns. It has more to do with naiveté, familial love and personal vigor. These are hardly negative ideas. Rural Mainers can rest assured. Nobody —no one worth a damn in any case— will think of rural Maine, central Maine, or whatever, as a shithole because of "Vacationland." Those who do are not necessarily elitists or hipsters. They're just superficial. And superficial people come in all forms.

**

February, 29, 2012: Socialitelife.com catches pop star Rihanna coming out of a posh London establishment. Seventeen photos of the "event" are posted online. Rihanna is wearing a faded denim shirt, an oversized trucker hat, studded white hot pants, tacky thigh-high leather boots, purple lipstick, dark sunglasses, three cheap-looking necklaces, and gilded hoop earrings. Under her left earring there's a neck tattoo with the words "rebelled fleur," written in the kind of cursive handwriting formerly associated with jail gangs. Her bleached, frizzy hair is kept in a haphazard ponytail, under which darker roots are not only shown, but flaunted. A tall man in a suit who is perhaps her bodyguard, stands behind her at all times; fans stand in front. The caption by the photos reads, "Rihanna Goes White Trash Chic."

Picture this craziness. A Barbados-born singer is visiting London dressed like a poor, rural American (or what some style advisor or clothing designer imagines poor, rural Americans look like). The security guard, on the other hand, is wearing a blue suit. The fans are wearing regular clothes too. Only Rihanna, the star, looks "trailer park chic," "blue collar couture," or whatever. It's just fashion, sure, but thinking of this trend as a mere fashion style doesn't do justice to its wide reach. Fashion is the focal point, but poor, rural America-inspired culture has already bled into areas like television, music, literature, interior design and even architecture.

It's impossible to pinpoint the exact time when the trend went mainstream. It goes back to at least the early 2000s. As with many "edgy" trends, it probably started within a few creative clusters and then caught on with the wider public, until eventually, clothing corporations helped globalize it. Seeing kids today walking around the streets of Tokyo or São Paulo dressed as struggling rural Americans is the most normal thing in the world, even if they, as the Nirvana song goes, "know not what it means." Talking about Nirvana, the same happened with grunge in the '90s. Old jeans, boots and faded flannel shirts were the staple style of the Pacific Northwest working class, including alternative musicians and fans. After the local music scene became famous, the grunge look went global, even couture, before it finally faded away.

The "white trash" look has spread far beyond

countercultural clusters, so it can't last too much longer. For now, though, it is still around. Here's an ad for what sounds like a wonderful club in Florida: "Redneck cool. Trailer-park fabulous. White-trash chic. Blue-collar vogue. Whatever you wish to call it, it is hip and it's fun with a downtown vibe. With great promotions and parties, live music, 32 huge TV's, a full delicious menu and a ton of cool people to meet every day, *Whiskey Tango* gives you something to do and a place to hang 7 days a week!" Whiskey Tango is code language, of course. Whiskey stands for white and Tango for trash. Going trashy is a commercially attractive model. New Times Magazine has voted Whiskey Tango "best bar" in Broward and Palm Beach.

Corporations also go nuts for seemingly authentic cultural trends. When a corporation's branding apparatus grabs a hold of a cultural trend, it goes all out and stays seamless at the same time. Levi's 2010 "Go Forth" campaign, handled by famed advertising agency Wieden + Kennedy comes to mind. One TV ad shows working class youngsters walking around a struggling rural town. Fireworks go off as a rare wax cylinder recording of Walt Whitman reading his poem "America" plays in the background. Yes, the real Walt Whitman reading from Leaves of Grass is featured in a Levi's ad with the sole purpose of bestowing authenticity upon a brand. It was a way to honor the brand's so-called birthright. "Shot on location in Braddock, the campaign features a dozen residents of diverse backgrounds dressed in Levi's® Work Wear Collection for fall," a Levi's press release said. "Work wear is Levi's® birthright."

Top to bottom examples of rural poor inspiration abound; think Ed Hardy, Megan Fox, Kid Rock, "My

Name is Earl," and Trailer Park Boys. But street-level life shows how assimilated the trend has become. Things like cheap beer, trucker hats, mustaches, "wife beaters," beards, greasy hair and even beer bellies are worshiped (ironically, but worshiped nonetheless) in many non-poor, non-rural quarters. I've been told that some of the most sophisticated women in Silverlake, hip-central Los Angeles, will not go out on a date with a guy unless he has a broken tooth and is wearing a Lynyrd Skynyrd T-shirt with cut-out sleeves.

**

Hinterland: "A region remote from urban areas; backcountry. A region situated beyond metropolitan centers of culture."

The American hinterlands have become precious because they are fading. They are fading because that's the way of the country; the way of development, growth, expansion, late capitalism, whatever you want to call it. Someday this vast continent will be one giant asphalt block, swarming with urban or suburban dwellers. In this sense the American hinterlands — though one imagines the same thing is happening in China and Russia— are precious in the same way that dying languages are precious. Dying languages need to be recorded and studied because they present a unique way of looking at the world, a different filter. Dying subcultures, like the one shown in "Vacationland," do too.

That said, in his best photos Steven Rubin goes beyond documentation. He reaches intimacy with his subjects by treating them like family. He comes closer to Richard Billingham taking photos of his own alcoholic father and obese mother in the powerful photo book *Ray's A Laugh* than to Dorothea Lange recording the plight of poor Americans for the Farm Security Administration during the 1930s. In Billingham, tenderness cancels out much of the judgment; the photos turn the stomach, but warm up the heart too. The same happens in "Vacationland."

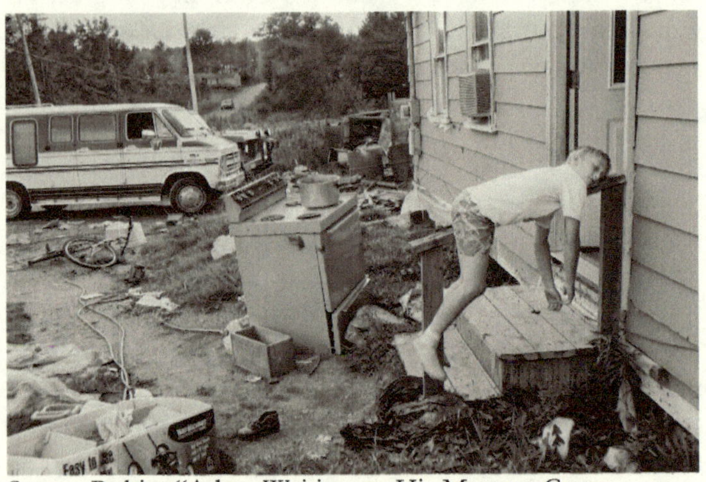

Steven Rubin. "Adam Waiting on His Mom to Come Home." 2001.

Stomachs are turned by the terrible living standards. But what warms up the heart? The raw visual poetry? Well, not really. Of course many of Rubin's images are beautiful. The most beautiful one is "Adam Waiting on His Mom to Come Home." Asleep on the railing like some type of exotic bird perched on a branch, Adam's little soul is a million miles away, floating above the front yard junk (and all the socioeconomic realities that junk entails). Even so, lyricism is not the most salient feature of "Vacationland." The idea of longing is. Not the subjects' longing. Polly with the "Born To Die" tattoos, Tracy with the cat, Rena and Everett under the Elvis poster, Laura Ann with her dad and rifle, and Ernie with his wheel couldn't care less about you and me. We are the ones in a gallery staring at frozen frames of apparently worse off strangers. "Vacationland" can reflect back our own cultural longing. That's what's moving about it.

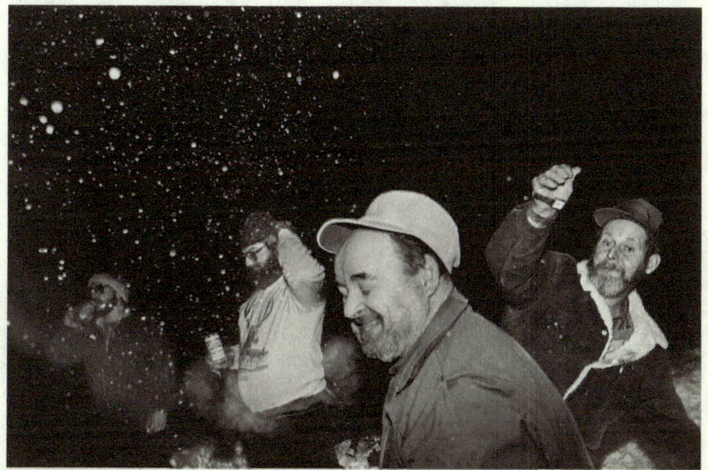

Steven Rubin. "Celebrating Christmas Night Out on the Frozen Bog." 1992.

Take "Celebrating Christmas Night Out on the Frozen Bog." These four might not be the most successful or most handsome of men. They are ragged (really ragged, not "trailer trash chic" ragged) and quite possibly smelly and drunk. Two of them are drinking a brand of beer that's quite possibly not Stella Artois. The two on the left look utterly relaxed; the two on the right, fucking blissful. In their crazy abandon they look like wasted teenagers at a punk rock concert. Not too many urban or suburban men in their 50s or 60s (or any post-college age really) can pull this off. Many wish they could.

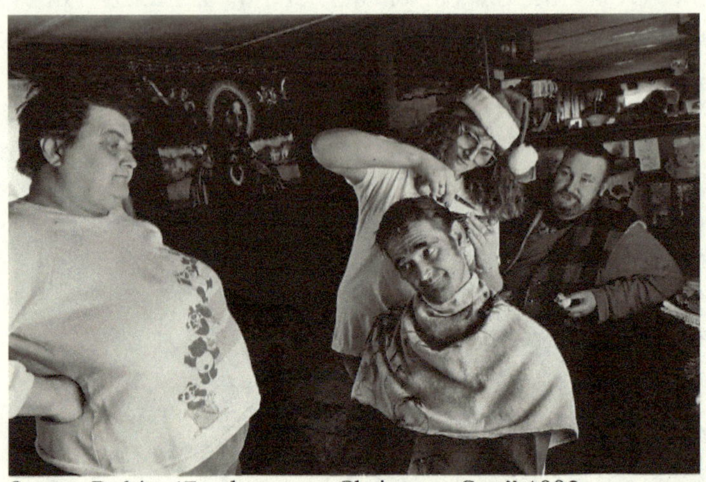

Steven Rubin. "Lucky gets a Christmas Cut." 1992.

Then there's "Lucky Gets a Christmas Cut." The woman in the Santa hat might not be the best hairstylist in the world. And the wall art isn't precisely Gagosian Gallery material (well, you never know). The point is, this might not even be an actual hair salon. It's probably somebody's house. But three adults are engrossed in the action. It's just a haircut, but look at their faces. They may as well be watching the NBA finals. The man getting the haircut would be right to consider himself the most appreciated man alive. I'm sure every person in that room knows each other's name and even what each one likes to have for dinner. You can almost see fraternity linking these people like a pink ribbon around a Christmas gift.

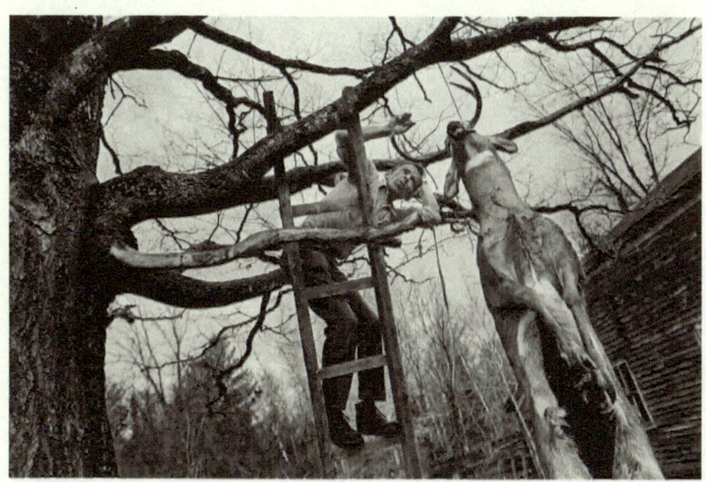

Steven Rubin. "Hanging Deer." 1994.

In "Hanging Deer" we learn that the man in the photo, or somebody in his circle, killed that poor animal. The deer could have and should have been spared. But if all cultural judgments are put aside, a silent vigor comes through. The vigor is not so much in the photo itself, but in its context. The story surrounding the photo is full of adventure, rituals and a deep connection to the land. Also, there's a sense of real accomplishment. Real blood, real rifles, real killing. It's the opposite of, for instance, Facebook reality. There's no physical detachment in "Vacationland"'s world. To be up by that dead deer, you need to trudge through the cold mud, get on your knees and pull that trigger. Then you need to drag the animal to the truck, drive it home and hang it from a branch. No password or browser will ever grant you access to that reality.

Why does Rihanna wear a trucker hat around London? Why is a Florida bar called Whiskey Tango? Why does a Levi's ad flaunt shoddy Pennsylvanian houses? Why do hipsters grow mullets? The short answer: because terrorists don't attack trailer parks. The long answer: take sustained look at the photographs.

Almagul Menlibayeva

Russia conquered Kazakhstan in the 18th century. By 1936, that vast Middle Asian country had become a Soviet republic. This means that for most of the 20th century, indigenous Kazakhstani culture was "de-emphasized" in favor of Soviet culture. Russian became the country's official language and communism the official system. The loaded term "cultural genocide" has been employed. This much is certain: for several decades, a set of cultures was forcibly repressed in favor of a foreign ideology. Call it what you will; the scars are still there.

Kazakhstan became independent in 1991. Discarding the Soviet ways and going back to Kazakhstani culture seemed like the natural next step. The dilemma is that Soviet immigration policies had shifted the country's ethnic makeup. Nowadays ethnic Kazakhs make up only about 60 percent of the population. Russians, Uzbeks, Ukrainians and others make up the rest. Russian is spoken by over 90 percent of the people and has remained the country's intercultural language.

Finding a common Kazakh mythology for citizens to gather around seems difficult, to say the least. And yet Almagul Menlibayeva is giving it a try. Why?

Performance artists have a penchant for herculean acts. Also, her quest fulfills a personal need.

Here's what she said about self-identity during a recent interview: "People born in the Soviet Union, we don't know our past. I learned traditions when I went to my grandmother's village. But in the village you notice only the rituals and everyday behavior. The intellectual information, you cannot get because, it's very sad to say, but during collectivization, during the '30s, there were a lot of people who died, moved, and ran away from the communists. [It was hard] to get information about who you are, from where you came and why. There was a big gap. I used to say: I'm a modern person, but who am I?"

Here the idea of atavism emerges. Atavism is the recurrence in a plant or an animal of certain primitive characteristics that were present in an ancestor but have not occurred in intermediate generations; it is a reversion to a former or more primitive type. In her art, Menlibayeva continuously invokes her ancient self. She looks for it around the Kazakh steppe. This is a huge grassy area that was first populated by Turkic nomads before the Arabs arrived in the eighth century (Mongols joined in during the 13th century). Now, it would be dishonest for me to pretend to understand who these Islamic, Turkic and Mongol nomads really are. It's enough to know that Tengrism —a Central Asian religion characterized by shamanism, animism, totemism, polytheism and ancestor worship— was integral in the development of Central Asian nomadic culture.

"Who am I?" Almagul Menlibayeva asks.

She was born in 1969 in Almaty, Kazakhstan's largest city, and attended Academy of Art and Theater of Albaty. At first she was a painter, but eventually found her way to performance art, photography and video art. She's a fashionable, dark-haired woman, who wears thick-framed glasses, speaks English, and calls herself a nomad. But she doesn't gallop through the endless steppes on horseback looking for animals to sacrifice. She works the Albaty, Berlin, and New York gallery circuits. She's not a steppe nomad, but then again, here is where her atavism crystallizes: her rituals invoke the nomadic world. In her best work she seems to stand in the middle of her own dreams, changed.

Instead of inserting herself into an ancient mythological realm, however, Menlibayeva's art brings the mythological world out into the present (that is, globalization and post-modernity). Menlibayeva's videos and photos show strange images of goddesses that could have been taken from an Alejandro Jodorowski movie, but they also use editing techniques influenced by the MTV music video aesthetic. The sound effects she uses could have come out of any Hollywood horror movie. Her long legged models would not be out of place in Vogue. In terms of artistic language, Menlibayeva is as accessible as, to use two extreme examples, Cindy Sherman and David LaChapelle. But that's just the bait. Almagul Menlibayeva's metaphysics are destined to remain impenetrable.

This serves a purpose. Traditionally, Western artists have been attracted to Orientalism for various reasons, but it has mostly come down to a search for freshness. That's fine, but being fetishistic (or just fake) is a constant danger for those artists who go too far in their foreign expeditions. The opposite is also true. Non-

Western art can be either unapproachable or too self-consciously derivative of Western forms. Menlibayeva has devised a cunning system. Her tools are Western, but she uses those tools then to dig down underneath her own feet. The outcome is rare: uncontrived exotic art.

Aldo Tambellini's Lanterna Magica

My cell phone rang at midnight. It was Anna Salamone, telling me Aldo Tambellini —the poet, painter and video art pioneer— was now ready to talk. I had spoken with Salamone, the artist's curator and companion, several times before, but not with Tambellini.

"You can call me Aldo. I'm not into formalities or anything like that," he said.

He was open and had a hearty laugh. I quickly forgot I was talking to an 80-year-old man whose most celebrated experimental videos and films were shot in New York's Lower East Side during the '60s and '70s, long before I was born.

The fact is Aldo Tambellini has been madly churning out art pieces ever since he was a child in pre-WWII Italy. Unless he's feeling ill or weak, he is probably painting or writing a poem as you read this.

Perhaps remaining out of the mainstream for decades has instilled in him a young artist's zest for creation, as if he were perpetually starting off. Perhaps it's been something else.

That's what I wanted to track down: the source of his almost religious commitment to art.

The first couple of nights we spoke over the phone until around 3 a.m. After that, despite worsening health problems, he agreed to meet me personally in Cambridge, the town he reluctantly calls home.

II. *Across the Atlantic, Across the Years*

In 1932, Giovanni and Gina Tambellini and their two children (5-year-old Paul and 2-year-old Aldo) took a ship back to Italy. New York, or the broken American dream, was left behind.

At age 6, pleurisy, water in the lungs, struck Aldo. He spent several months in bed. "My mother was very intelligent. You can see in the photographs, a very beautiful woman." She bought him art books, a marionette theatre and a kind of projector with batteries called *lanterna magica.* Eventually Aldo got better. He started writing plays for his marionettes and projecting little clips of film in his *lanterna magica.* When he turned 10, Gina contacted Instituto d'Arte Augusto Passaglia, where he began to take classical studio art classes.

Lucca, founded by the Etruscans and known as the city of art and music, was the perfect place for a young artist. The city preserves the Roman street plan, medieval basilicas and Renaissance frescos.

But when Aldo was a child, Mussolini was in power. War incinerated the sky.

One night at 4 a.m. Aldo had to hide in a cornfield,

between furrows. German soldiers were firing machine guns in his direction. Another time, a bomb fell in front of his house, killing 21 neighbors. Such were his formative years.

In 1946, 16-year-old Aldo and Gina boarded The Marine Carp, a Red Cross evacuation ship. Aldo's father, Giovanni, had already moved back to New York. His older brother, Paul, had joined the American military. "It was my brother's idea [to go back to America]. I didn't want to come. My brother was very conformist."

Sixteen days later, after a long and feverish trip across the Atlantic, the Marine Carp docked in New York City on the Fourth of July. "My father looked younger than me. I wrote a poem about this. I felt a lot older than 16. The war experience had taken its toll."

America felt strange, ugly and impenetrable. Aldo didn't speak English and the new landscape looked nothing like Lucca with its red clay roofs and 16th century walls. And, of course, that very same day, that one conversation: Giovanni wanted a separation from Gina. Aldo was shocked and that much more confused.

"America made no sense to me. I could not connect at all."

Aldo and Gina settled alone in Syracuse, New York.

But some lights shone at home. Gina was afraid. She feared there might be hidden microphones somewhere. She feared the Gestapo would come to America and snatch Paul and Aldo away from her. She feared those lights at home More and more and so Aldo had to contact Rochester State Hospital. They gave Gina electroshock. Beautiful, intelligent Gina.

That was the end of something.

After that, Aldo got a scholarship at Syracuse

University. Something else opened up: Syracuse University, Oregon University, Notre Dame. And then, in the summer of 1959, he rented a place on the Lower East Side for $56 a month. It looked like a bombed-out area from World War II. In that rubble he found inspiration.

III. *Through the Looking Lens*

New York City, 1967: An old TV set appears on the black and white screen. A small white light moves frantically inside the screen. The strong, dry voice of a news reporter from the '60s presents Aldo Tambellini as part of a series of reports about the East Village.

"Aldo Tambellini was one of the first artists to work in the East Village. He is soon to open a show utilizing videotape. He calls it a media explosion. He plans to surround his audience with TV receivers in total darkness," the reporter says, in a tense tone, as if reporting from a crime scene.

The camera pans to the left. Tambellini stands behind a video console, a big machine similar to a DJ table. He looks intense, wearing all black. The videotape is wrapped around two reels, making two circles reminiscent of 78 RPM records. Tambellini looks like a video DJ, playing some kind of abstract, frantic visual music.

"The artist will have to get to this medium and begin to explore the possibilities," a 37-year-old Tambellini says. "After all, to me, television, what is it? It is actually an image made out of light, which travels in time and space. It is the same energy we have discovered through atoms."

He speaks fast and emphatically, in a thick Italian

accent, moving his body forward.

"It is the same energy which we are now discovering through light. And when creative people begin to get involved with this idea of energy, rather than with the idea of making pictures for a certain people," he says, his arms going up to his chest and then strongly down, "when artists begin to say, 'We are making forms for everybody, we are exploring possibilities for everybody,' then we will come to some creative aspect which will not belong to one particular class, but it will be a new exploration, which is for everybody."

The camera zooms in on the television screen once again: a little flame, something like a comet or sperm moves on the screen, creating light spirals. There's a high, muffled sound, like a telephone line or an alien flying through space. A kind of supernova fills up the screen and then something like a bubble or a womb develops. A few beeps are heard as on a life-support machine. The little flame splits into two, moves around playfully, and then disappears, leaving behind nothing but a black screen.

"Is it art?" asks the newscaster in his forensic tone.

A pause and then the ruthless conclusion.

"It's what passes for art in the East Village. Tomorrow, a final look at this community. John Parsons reporting."

IV. *Bittersweet Home: Cambridge, Massachusetts*

Aldo Tambellini and Anna Salamone offered to pick me up. I waited in the parking lot of the Super 8 Motel, not really knowing what they looked like. I was a little surprised when I first saw Tambellini. I expected a younger man. Not that he looked any older than his age, but over the phone his voice and engagement were those of a man 30 or 40 years younger.

He was wearing a red bandana around his neck, sported a rat-tail, had a leather bracelet around his wrist, and carried a cane with a horse carved on the handle. It felt as if I was visiting my long-lost, hip, socialist grandfather.

We went to Casa Portugal, one of Tambellini's favorite restaurants. The waiter put the *paella Valenciana* on the left, but Anna said to put it on the right so she could assist Tambellini. He started talking about life in the '50s.

"The Mills Brothers Circus had around a 1,000 people that traveled from small town to small town outside of Syracuse. I borrowed a camera from a friend of a friend and went to take pictures of the circus," he said. "Once there, I asked if I could join them and sketch and photograph the activities. [Mr. Mills] assigned me to the clowns and midgets to live with."

There was a dim underlying point in his anecdote. This is something Tambellini does all the time. He digresses and circumvents around the main point of a story, or he lays out a cluster of stories, but understates the connections or leaves the point unsaid.

Artists were more committed in the past. They had a vision. And they did crazy things like joining a circus. Not anymore. Today's art world is full of mercenaries and fakes. That was his point. Or one of his points, in any case.

Tambellini dislikes the direction contemporary art took after Andy Warhol. Pop culture and detachment are not part of his sensibility. Instead, he values political engagement, seriousness and a kind of secular religiosity. He has an inclination to tackle big questions:

death, morality, freedom and the purpose of life.

Anna, a retired Italian-American school administrator from Connecticut, 17 years Tambellini's junior, nodded her head at everything Tambellini said, always looking at him with tenderness and awe.

"It was like sitting at the feet of a master, just listening to him," she said about the first time she heard him speak. "I imagined what it would have been like to sit with Sophocles or Dante."

Anna and Tambellini met through a friend about nine years ago. She now dedicates several hours a day to everything from making sure he stays healthy to promoting his work.

"The man is productive!" she said, proudly claiming to have typed 1,205 of Tambellini's poems, so far.

We stayed at Casa Portugal until closing time and then drove to a nearby café Tambellini likes because it stays open late. MIT, a school Tambellini has deep connections with, is a few blocks away. A fellowship at MIT's Center for Advanced Visual Studies brought Tambellini to Cambridge in 1978. He moved there from Brooklyn with his life-companion Sara Dickinson, whose death in 1996 of alcohol-related liver problems sent him to a mental hospital twice.

Tambellini's friend Bharat Bhatt, a retired geography and theology professor from India, happened to be at the café. We ordered tea and sat outside. It started getting a little windy. The wind is not good for Tambellini's right eye, which itches and burns and fills up with tears.

But the man is tireless.

He started talking about how when he was a kid in Italy he used to sit in front of the radio and listen to the few transmitted shows. We all listened in silence as he talked in minute detail about the advent of the telegram and the telephone, fax machines and newspapers, cinema and television, and computers and the Internet.

The wind kept blowing and tears started rolling down Tambellini's right cheek.

Employees began to clean up around the patio.

Tambellini then said something negative about Boston, but we had been sitting there for a couple of hours and it was getting cold.

"Have you ever thought of moving back to Italy?" I asked.

There was a short pause. A young employee told us we had to go.

Anna leaned forward and eagerly spoke: "Tell him why you don't move back to Italy, Aldo."

Tambellini remained quiet for a second. I thought I'd asked the wrong question and tried to make eye contact with Bhatt, but he was texting somebody, falling asleep, or looking at something on the floor. It was well past 2 a.m.

"Because it is too beautiful," Tambellini said, a little sad. "Italy is just too beautiful."

Notes: Arthur Nersesian's *The Fuck Up*

So I've picked my top ten fiction books of all time and decided to re-read each one of them. The plan is to do close readings of each book, chapter by chapter, if possible. This is going to take months. To get started I'm just looking at one book's beginning.

The Fuck Up (1997), written by Arthur Nersesian, opens up with a sort of false truism: "Perhaps the price of comfort is that life passes more rapidly. But for anyone who has lived in uneasiness, even for a short, memorable duration, it's a trade-off that will gladly be made."

Those first sentences remind me of how *Pride and Prejudice* starts, though Jane Austen's turn of phrase is more graceful. "It is a truth universally acknowledged that a single man in possession of a good fortune must be in want of a wife."

Both novels open with the narrator stating a general truth that sounds like the last word on something, but in reality it is anything but.

Right after the first sentence, *The Fuck Up*'s unnamed narrator constricts his scope, going from general truth to a sort of abstract/detached description of his past: "When I was in my teens I made an appraisal of how comfortable my life could turn out when I became the age I am now. Because of a mechanical failure, the prediction is inexact. Things reversed."

He then narrows it down even more, getting to actual facts: "I ended up living somewhere I once avoided, with a woman whom I once genuinely disliked."

So the narrator's life, which was supposed to turn out good, "got fucked" because of a "mechanical failure." Life sucks.

That was the first paragraph. The narrator seems self-consciously negative, but not self-pitying. The novel's tone is too ironic for that.

The second paragraph brings in a twist that advances the narrator's bitterness: "Recently we celebrated our seventh anniversary together with a decent dinner and a not-dreadful film."

So seven years later, his life is still fucked, though not utterly.

That sets up the whole novel. Then the narrator goes into flashback mode to explain just exactly how his life went wrong.

**

As much as I love *The Fuck Up*, it struggled to get on my top ten list. Françoise Sagan's *Bonjour Tristesse* had its place before the final cut. *The Fuck Up* isn't like the other books on my list. It's the lightest and most readable one. I remember it as a very good novel, not a masterpiece. Also, as opposed to every other writer on my list, I've never obsessed over the author, Arthur Nersesian. I haven't even read any of his other novels.

And yet, man did *The Fuck Up* shake me up to the core when I first read it. I want to say I was about 22 or 23, pretty much the same age as the novel's protagonist. I had just dropped out of UC Berkeley, my girlfriend had broken up with me when I came back from Berkeley to Los Angeles, and my closest cousin —who was just 16— had died in a car accident in Indiana. I, too, at least in my head, was a fuck up with aimless but burning literary ambitions. It's all becoming clearer now.

**

I'm almost done re-reading with *The Fuck Up*. Writing observations about it chapter by chapter, as I'd planned, required more commitment than I have. I filled the book with writing in the margins, but instead of posting my notes, I just kept reading. Here are some general impressions. There will be more. This novel, after all, influenced the hell out of me when I was a college kid.

But I'm not blind. *The Fuck Up* has many technical flaws. Worst of all, there's an over reliance on co-incidences. Sure, the plot moves along swiftly and there's always something going on, which is good, but on too many occasions it just feels like Nersesian goes back to a bad habit: inserting unlikely coincidences to get things going. He's like a doctor who goes for the defibrillator very time a patient needs CPR. You can't do that.

Another flaw: most of the novel's secondary characters are one-dimensional. Even some of the main characters suffer from this.

And the turn of sentence is rough, even for an underground, dark-humor cult novel.

Still, I fully understand why I loved this book so much when I first read it. Actually, I still love it. I get a feeling that Nersesian enjoyed writing it like few writers enjoy writing their novels; this comes through in almost every sentence. *The Fuck Up* is Nersesian's tale. He owns every part of it. You can almost see him enjoying the dark literary references and laughing at his characters' scatological jokes. When he digresses, he seems to do so because he feels like it. I respect that. A coming-of-age story that pretends to encapsulate a particular time and place (the lower East Side in the '80s) and a particular worldview (that of a sort of East Coast slacker with literary ambitions) has to be personal. Well, "The Fuck Up" is as personal as a diary entry.

It must be tough to write a novel with such a strong voice. Exposing your views to the world hoping that they turn out to be less like prejudices and more like a generation's shared moral outlooks takes guts. If you pull it off all the way, you end up with *The Catcher in the Rye* or with *On the Road;* if not, you end up with yet another embarrassingly confessional narrative. If you pull it off, but not all the way, you end up with *The Fuck Up*, which some readers love and other don't get at all.

Nersesian's voice is gritty, literary, impure, male and street smart. I see the novel as a kind of updated and more personal *Bright Lights Big City*. Why didn't *Bright Lights Big City* by Jay McInerney make it into my top ten? Because I read it just a couple of years ago. And being 28 is nothing like being 22. Books, like music, have a different impact depending on how old you are. You have to read a book at the right time for it to become part of your self-perception.

**

Here are the ten fiction books that have influenced me the most. Many of these books (and their writers) I've been obsessed with for years at a time. They are not the books I would critically say are the best I've read. They are just the most influential on a personal level. These books have not only impacted my own fiction, but personality and even life choices. One day I hope to write an essay about each one and publish the collected essays as a book.

10. *The Fuck Up*, Arthur Nersesian (1997, USA)
9. *Red and Black*, Stendhal (1830, France)
8. *The Immoralist*, André Gide (1925, France)
7. *Crime and Punishment*, Fyodor Dostoyevski (1866, Russia)
6. *Los Detective Salvajes*, Roberto Bolaño (2008, Chile)
5. *The Work (So Far)*, Deborah Eisenberg (1997, USA)
4. *The Nick Adams Stories*, Ernest Hemingway (1972, USA)
3. *Los Siete Locos/ Los Lanzallamas*, Roberto Arlt (1929; 1931, Argentina)
2. *Ficciones*, Borges Luis Borges (1944, Argentina)
1. *The Daring Young Man on the Flying Trapeze*, William Saroyan (1934, USA)

Roberto Arlt's *Mad Toy*

I read about early 20th century Argentinean writer Roberto Arlt a couple of months ago in an interview given by the late Chilean writer Roberto Bolaño, whose translated novels are beginning to appear in English in New Directions. In the interview, Bolaño said that no one read Roberto Arlt anymore. So I made a mental note to pick up something by Arlt, but then, as most of my mental notes go, I forgot.

Or so I thought. A couple of weeks ago I was in the Spanish section of the Central Library in Los Angeles looking for god knows what when I somehow stumbled upon three of Arlt's novels in Spanish: *El juguete babioso*, (Mad Toy), *Los siete locos* (The Seven Madmen) and *Los lanzallamas* (The Flame Throwers). I picked up *Los Siete Locos* and read the prologue by Juan Carlos Onetti, the Uruguayan writer. Onetti praised Arlt in a way that made it hard not to check out the book. He said that Arlt was the "closest thing to genius" to ever come out of the Río de la Plata. I thought about Jorge Luis Borges and Julio Cortázar and was surprised that Onetti had not mentioned them as being close to genius.

I was blown away by the novel mainly because of Arlt's use of language. He uses the whole of Spanish. This is kind of hard to explain. Though the characters are deeply Argentinean, and they speak the way Argentineans do, Arlt does not confine his language to Buenos Aires. He opens up his ear to the whole language of Latin America and Spain. You don't know whether the narrator's Mexican, Argentinean or Spanish. He mixes slang with scientific or intellectual words, neologisms with archaic terms and ready-made phrases with poetic metaphors of his own. It was astonishing. Arlt's Spanish might be baroque at times, but it is not literary at all. It feels alive. You can sense the genius.

The plot is simple. A group of lively and smart junior high students make a huge plan to rob their own school. The planning and actual execution brings them very close to each other. They pull it off for the most part, but at the end everything crumbles down and they go their separate ways in life. The reader stays with one of them, Silvio Astier, a kind of Julian Sorel, the main character from Stendhal's *The Red and Black*. Silvio is a tragic character. He tries to make it out of poverty but fails year after year because of how society is built.

Harsh reality pushes Silvio to deal with the worst of urban Buenos Aires: grotesque characters for whom there is nothing beyond money and satisfying their crudest sensual needs. Throughout the novel Silvio has to deal with an exasperating dilemma. He wants to make quick money to bring his mother and sister out of poverty, but also needs to give meaning to his life. He needs an outlet, any outlet, for self-expression and existential fulfillment.

At one point, after having made it through hell, he

gets kicked out of the Air Force for being "too much of a thinker." This destroys his aspirations because he had put all of his energy into the Air Force. He tries to kill himself but fails. At this point he meets a good-hearted parking attendant who lets him know of his plan to rob a rich man's house with the help of the man's maid. This is Silvio's last shot at making money. Everything seems to be about to work out perfectly when something completely unforeseen happens. Shit. The reader is taken aback and then the novel's over. "What the hell!" the reader thinks and throws the book against the wall while cursing at both Roberto Arlt and Silvio Astier.

But then you think about it and, little by little, begin to see what it was all about. You pick up the book from the floor and apologize because you realize that Arlt's point was something else altogether. And you also realize that Silvio was much more complex than you thought. Then you go back to the library and pick up Arlt's second novel, *Los siete locos* (Seven Madmen) in Spanish and it changes your life forever.

Homoeroticism in "America's Finest Kids"

Sometimes photography does not need ideas. It does not need to "build bridges," "explore worlds" or even "document reality." Photography has a scientific vein that allows it to skirt the art world's confining rhetoric. There's a long history of this. Think, for instance, of Eadweard Muybridge's 19th century motion and anatomy experiments. Their aim was not artistic.

Nowadays, photo portraiture in particular can be free of rhetoric because in it a man can be a man and a woman can be a woman. In Terry Smith's exhibit, "America's Finest Kids," a naked young man without an inch of fat in his body is just that. Try seeing Picasso's "Les Demoiselles d'Avignon" as nothing more than five prostitutes if you can. Only photography has that ability.

And yet, as straightforward as the images in "America's Finest Kids" are, a lot is up to the viewer. This is true about all art experiences, but much more so in this case. Smith's photos showcase a very particular kind of homoeroticism: older eyes lusting after the young —too young really— male body. Obviously, the show might be too risqué for some people.

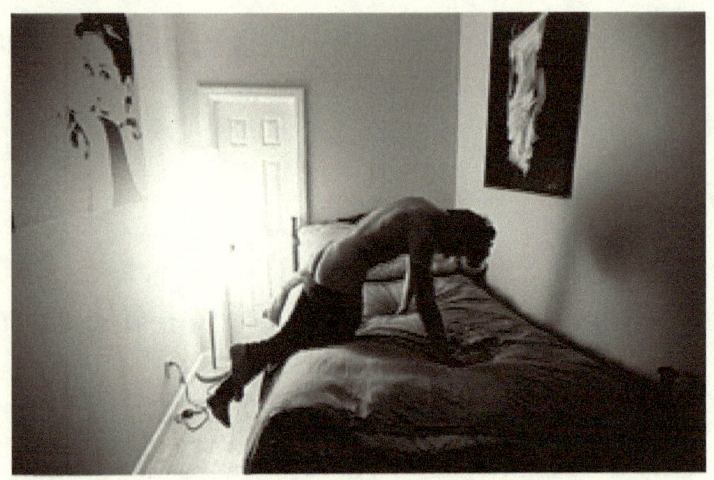

Terry Smith. From "America's Finest Kids."

Viewers can focus, I guess, on the photographs' aesthetic and social values instead. A person who is not into young beach-dwelling men can, for instance, look at the way the sunset lights up a face. You can add that the photos show some telling elements of California youth culture: skateboards, teenage haircuts, tattoos and piercings. And that the viewer can look at nonsexual elements like model selection, postures, lighting, angles and locations. You can argue that the photos can offer much more besides sex.

There's something to that, but I don't really buy it. Those who can't look at Terry Smith's photos with lust will probably miss 90 percent of what they have to offer.

"America's Finest Kids" is a collection of lust

triggers. Everything else is secondary. Even Smith's own goals and personal background seem secondary. Knowing that he was born into a Christian family in Oklahoma in 1962 and that he has been involved in helping at-risk youth in California, Haiti and other places doesn't add much to the experience. Knowing that his artistic goal is "to show that, despite their outward appearance, these 'damaged' kids are all beautiful" and that he "simply want[s] to celebrate the beauty and strength found in the American male" is almost distracting.

Again, one of the strengths of photography is that it can do away with rhetoric. In this case, dressing up such a "bare" group of images with social, anthropological or pseudo-literary aims obfuscates what's really there.

This brings me to my last point. "America's Finest Kids" is wrongly being called a photographic essay. The essay is a literary genre. In photography, the essay label is used as a metaphor to emphasize three aspects of a visual body of work: 1) its exploratory nature, 2) its short, narrow scope, and 3) its wish to make a tentative statement about a particular issue. "America's Finest Kids" does not do any of the three.

Smith has been photographing young men for 15 years. He has taken thousands of photographs. If we were to stick to literary metaphors, I would call it a sexual memoir of vast proportions. Because, come on now, "America's Finest Kids" isn't an exercise in anthropological documentation. Even when the young men are photographed in their own rooms, Smith somehow manages to pull them into his own hyper-sexualized realm. Smith never silently steps into the subject's world as a documentarian would. As a result, one ends up learning more about the photographer's sexual predilections than about the teens' lives.

The images are beautifully lit, well-composed and show a great gift for capturing young men right at the point between adolescence and manhood. The possibilities for a very particular kind of homoeroticism are there, but the viewer must first be able to synch up with Smith's questionable sexual gaze. I predict that many people will not go there. Ethics can be stronger than aesthetics.

Full woman, fleshly apple, hot moon,
thick smell of seaweed, crushed mud and light,
What obscure brilliance opens between your columns?
What ancient night does a man touch
with his senses?

Sonnet XII, Pablo Neruda

Staring into Vaginas: Camera Night at the Ivar

It was probably a Sunday in the '80s.

Three people stand out in the photograph; a man in a wheelchair with his back to the camera, a naked stripper above him on stage, and another man taking a photo. Something about the man in the wheelchair's body language spells out submission. His hands can't be seen, but they could well be clasped. I believe they are. The short man taking a photo is wearing black and has his back to the camera. Then there's the naked woman, the performer. She could be Barbie, Miss X, Silky, Angela, Hell's Angel, Aixa or any of the other girls who worked at the Ivar. She's obviously the focal point of the image, but she's more than part of the image's composition. She's a symbolic as well as an actual conduit for male lust. But this description isn't precise enough either.

Let's put it another way. Do you think the man in the wheelchair has an erection?

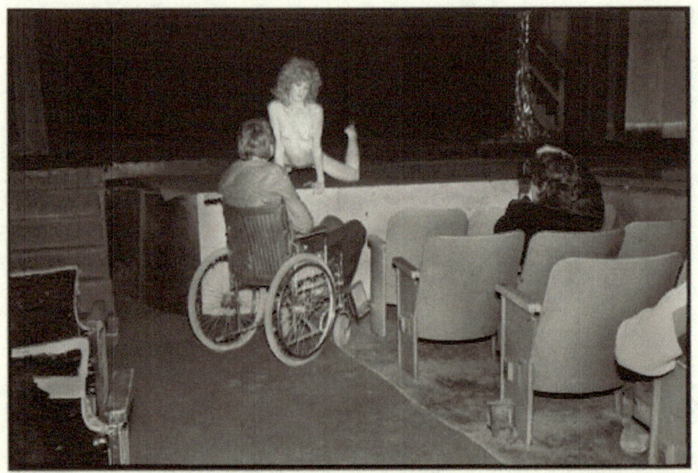

Ryan Herz. From "Camera Night at the Ivar." 1982.

It's possible that he does, though it's also possible that he doesn't. One thing we know for sure. At that very moment the photo is being taken, as the stripper contorts her body above him, the man is anywhere else but in his wheelchair. He's probably walking or running somewhere in his head; he might even be flying like a wild bird right above the Hollywood mountains. I believe that he is.

That's what this particular stripper is doing for her client. If you look at her body, her hair, and the whiteness of her skin, she resembles a bird or even a cherub more than a stripper. You almost expect her to pick him up by the shoulders and fly away.

It was probably a Sunday in the '80s.

Sunday was Bring Your Camera Night at the Ivar.

The small venue known as the Ivar Theater, built in 1950, is one of those Hollywood buildings with a special allure that has little to do with its rather mundane architecture. The mystique comes from what went on inside. During its first decade of existence it was a normal playhouse. Then it began to branch out. Elvis performed there in the 1957 film *Loving You.* Cult poet and comic Lord Buckley recorded a live album there in 1959. In the '60s, it became a rock venue. In 1966, The Grateful Dead recorded a crisp live album there. Then came a period when the venue switched owners constantly. In the mid '70s, it became a disreputable strip club with broken chairs and, as someone who'd been there put it, "cum-stained carpets."

Over time, the Ivar has taken on a kind of mythological life. Tom Waits went there in the '70s and mentions it in a least three of his songs. Playwright Ross MacLean wrote "Follies of Grandeur," a play performed in 2006, about the time he worked there. "A lot of the girls just danced around in street clothes, and took them off with about as much charm as someone undressing in a locker room. Pasties and G-strings were rare pleasures at the Ivar," he told The Tom Waits Library. The Ivar also came up in a 1983 Processed Word magazine essay by Linda Thomas, a former manager. "When someone in the audience started jerking off, the dancer would signal the projection booth and whoever was running the spotlight would focus it on him," she wrote.

So the Ivar was a quintessential Hollywood dump. Fante, Nathanael West, or Bukowski could have dreamed it up. (I bet at some point Bukowski actually found his way there). It was a place for the unluckiest, to borrow Joan Didion's label, "dreamers of the golden dream." At the Ivar, those dreamers eventually graduated into bitter survivalists, and the survivalists, into Hollywood rejects.

Photography, however, can make literary mythology problematic. Like writing, photos can help fictionalize reality, but unlike writing, photos bring measurable truth wherever they are displayed. That's where "Camera Night at the Ivar," the latest drkrm exhibit and catalog, comes in. Some now famous photographers such as Garry Winogrand shot there alongside the regulars. Because of this, lots of visual records of the Ivar at its most intimately pornographic exist. These photographs, both amateur and not, redirect the Ivar's mythology in a shocking way. They not only record the place's pornography, which is attractive in itself, but also capture —empirically so— fleeting moments of spiritual vigor.

Let's take a step back and look at the venue itself. What does a dark room with some working class men and a naked, economically desperate woman dancing on a stage mean? Any meaning will do, be it cultural, economic, historical or even oneiric. Actually, the oneiric meaning seems most appropriate here as it is the closest one to ritual. And, as British writer John Berger said in "Ev'ry Time We Say Goodbye," an essay comparing movies to other arts, "theatre brings actors before a public and every night during the season they re-enact the same drama. Deep in the nature of theatre is a sense of ritual return."

A strip club might be crude and sexually exploitative, but it is theater. The drama being re-enacted on a nightly basis is that of the possibilities and perils of coitus, where lust is the story line and the naked female is not the actor, but the stage. The only actor is the male customer. He pays his entrance fee so he can deliver a mute, oneiric monologue to himself.

The customer gets a deal because an erotic dream is a form of freedom. But a strip club is also a simple inhabited room. And any room, as French phenomenologist Gaston Bachelard said in his book "The Poetics of Space," is not dead space, but a dream-drawer. In fact, Bachelard thought that places inhabited by people could be read as psychological diagrams. He was particularly talking about rooms as described in certain poems, but the same case can be made about the poetics of photography.

Here are some conclusions I draw from looking at the Ivar Theater photographs:

A room is a womb; a stage is a window.

Lusting is daydreaming.

A naked woman on a stage always triggers a dream.

Daydreaming means escape. Transcendence.

For the human male, staring into a vagina is always a fascinating and a scary venture. He finds himself staring into a black hole, a bleeding wound, death, the origin and the end of life. There's an urge to touch, to taste, to penetrate. This is physical, of course, but, as the photos show, it isn't only naked flesh the lust-crazed male is after. Whether he knows it or not —whether by way of love, a prostitute or a stripper— the lust-crazed male is after that which the female flesh holds: empty space, metaphysics.

That's not to say photos ever cease to be historical documents. All the marks of time and the world are there: haircuts, clothes, décor, etc. Exploitation is also there. One can certainly lay out a litany of charges against these strip-club-going men. Many people will look at the Ivar photos that way, and they aren't wrong. But it should also be understood that these photos document more than that. The men in the "Camera Night at the Ivar" photos are so entranced, they may as well have been caught kneeling before an altar. That they have a hard-on and are flinging money at a degraded woman, who probably abhors being there, does not change matters.

POLITICS

Dispatch from the Immigration Trenches

Yes, times are tough for me too. Even though I recently graduated from a top journalism school, I had to take a job as a pizza delivery driver at Spumoni, an Italian restaurant in a wealthy L.A. neighborhood. I don't mind the gig because I get to meet a lot of interesting people and witness a lot of situations I wouldn't otherwise get to witness.

One day Victor, the main cook, one of the nicest and most responsible guys at the restaurant, came to work late. He usually gets to work before everyone else.

"*¿Qué pasó?*" I asked him.

We were outside, cleaning up. Victor took his time before replying.

"Last night a cop stopped me while driving on La Brea Boulevard because he thought I looked suspicious. And I didn't have a driver's license so he took my Honda Civic away."

Victor: shaved head, tattoos, baggy clothes. No working documents.

I couldn't say much, except *that sucks, man.*

We went into the kitchen and started getting things ready for the day ahead. Oscar, the other cook (an assertive, talkative guy with thick-framed glasses) already knew about the problem. He had some advice for Victor.

If you've ever worked at a restaurant you know that cooks treat each other with tenderness: "Let your fucking hair grow and stop wearing those damned baggy clothes."

Victor did not reply right away. In fact he didn't really reply. He muttered something later, but to himself while making bread with his hands: "But that is the way I dress…"

That is. The way. I dress. He stated it as a natural fact that cannot be altered such as one's height or eye color.

I understood his point and said something like *that's right, man.*

Oscar, however, was not having it. He turned to me and exclaimed out loud in a sarcastic tone.

"*Déjalo*, let him be. This fool wants this to happen again and again; maybe he has enough money to lose car after car."

During the last few years Victor has lost several cars to the police. Oscar, who is here legally, has helped him out time and again. It also happens Victor is sort of unlucky. That night there had been a gang shooting near La Brea and the cops were looking for drivers who fit a gang-member profile. He was asked for a license. He didn't have one. That's how he got his Honda Civic impounded. Unlucky stuff like this happens to people all the time. I know from experience.

But there's a second part to Victor's story, which is not as common.

That same night, after he got his car taken away,

while he was walking on the street, the cops stopped him *again*. Same reason: looks, style, fashion, cultural markers, whatever you want to call it.

I would have been furious.

Victor, who is totally laid back, saw the humor in it. "I told the cops I had been stopped earlier and had nothing else to donate to the police force," he said.

There isn't much more to say. Honda or no Honda, license or no license, I can only attest to the fact that Victor is a fast, polite cook, whose gnocchi and handmade bread are appreciated by many people in this mostly white Los Angeles neighborhood where Victor, Oscar and I work.

Here's something. The other day a customer said that Spumoni had changed the face of the neighborhood for the better. It was a simple but telling statement that got me thinking about simple but telling truths.

What makes a restaurant good?

By and large, it's food.

Food is at the heart of a restaurant. But even more than that. Food is at the heart of any society. The kitchen, not the living room, is the most important common room in any house.

Who makes food in a restaurant?

By and large, its employees. People.

Think of a pizza pie made in California. Who makes it happen? I've been there, so I can say. By and large, Spanish-speaking undocumented people pick the tomatoes in the fields, Spanish-speaking undocumented people make the dough and sauce, Spanish-speaking undocumented people wash the dishes, and Spanish-speaking undocumented people (or in my case, formerly undocumented people) deliver the pizzas. That's all I have to say.

Actually, there is something else, another little detail which Victor took a couple of days to share. You might find this last little detail crucial or anecdotal depending on how you see the world.

I have forgotten what exactly Victor was doing when he shared this little detail with me, but I can picture him in my head as he said it, thoughtful and sardonic as he is, washing a head of lettuce or spreading tomato paste over something.

I remember his words verbatim.

"The cop that took my car away told me I should be glad I was in California and not in Arizona because if I had been in Arizona, not only my car would have been taken away, but I would have also been deported back to Mexico."

How did the LAPD officer utter his words? Tone and inflection are key. The difference between empathy and degradation.

California is not Arizona or Alabama, but we live in the United States of America during the second decade of the 2000's. I have my theories.

Are We Going to Kill "Illegals"?

Rubén Luengas on undocumented immigrants

Los Angeles anchorman Rubén Luengas leads Telemundo's flagship local Hispanic news show, *En Contexto.* Besides having a knack for connecting with viewers on a personal level, Luengas can easily move back and forth between editorial and hard television news. In 2003, he won an Emmy for "The Forgotten," an in-depth story about dead undocumented immigrants whose unidentified bodies end up at the Los Angeles coroner's office. But he's also something of a Mexican Rachel Maddow. His biting questions and liberal comments have sparked some explosive reactions. The most notorious clash happened when former Mexican president Vicente Fox visited *En Contexto* to promote his book, "Revolution of Hope." Luengas, who had originally voted for Fox only to become utterly disillusioned, allowed room for little promotional chatter and instead stabbed Fox with probing questions about the slow-growing Mexican economy and, what ignited the blast, claims that Fox owned secret properties in Mexico. Fox ended up calling Luengas a slanderer and a vulgar idiot before storming out of the studio. The cameras were still rolling.

When you search for Vicente Fox on YouTube, the Luengas interview comes out on top. It's a kind of poetic victory for the journalist. But that was a few years ago, which is ages in television journalism time. Since the passing of the SB 1070 —a state law which gives policemen immigration enforcement in Arizona—immigration has become *En Contexto*'s ground zero. Luengas often reports from Arizona or speaks strongly against the law from the studio.

My sense is that Los Angeles' Hispanic immigrants see in Luengas not only as a journalist, but also a kind of political leader. The following scene has stayed in my head ever since I saw it unfold last May 1 during the immigration reform march in downtown Los Angeles. Former Los Angeles mayor Antonio Villaraigosa and other leaders were up on the podium speaking in broken Spanish about the need to legalize undocumented immigrants. Luengas, standing at a parking lot off to the side, was talking to a small group of people about the same thing, but in his crisp Spanish full of colloquialisms and unexpected turns of phrase. A short woman approached him out of the blue, her back to the podium.

"Luengas is the only person who speaks out for immigrants!" she said, overcome with emotion. People started clapping.

I decided to interview Luengas because he seems to speak for people who, either because of fear, difficulties with the dominant language or lack of education, cannot speak for themselves. I also wanted to know if he was for real.

I e-mailed him and, to my surprise, he e-mailed me back right away with his cell phone number. I called him and he said to come over to the Telemundo 52 studios in Burbank. He seemed happy and wired as we walked from room to room in the studios, talking with makeup artists, producers, a camera man and myself, whom he teasingly called "a very important journalist from a very important magazine."

After Luengas taped a promo without using a teleprompter, which might explain his signature free-flowing syntax, we walked to the back of the building, sat on the stairs for lack of chairs, and spoke about immigration for about 40 minutes. "The question is, what are we going to do with the world's poor? Are we going to kill them? Are we going to jail them? What are we going to do?" he asked during our interview. The spirit of that question summarizes my impression of this tall, blondish man who wears small oval-shaped glasses, jokes around with everyone, plays the piano and is given to reflect on the life of Christ. He would argue with a drunken bum on the street if the opportunity presented itself. And he'd probably do it using the same words he uses on live television. He *is* for real.

PM: Hi Rubén. Let's play a little game. I'll tell you 10 arguments against undocumented immigrants and you tell me your opinion in a few words.

RL: Sure.

PM: One: This country was built by laws.

RL: The U.S. has broken international law repeatedly (and I'm sorry, but I can't make it too short). For instance, there are a lot of Guatemalan immigrants in Los Angeles. Why? That's directly linked to an immoral, criminal and illegal act by Eisenhower's government in 1954 when the U.S. overthrew the Guatemalan president Jacobo Arbenz because he put in place an agrarian reform to help Guatemalan peasants. The U.S. started to label Arbenz as a communist and backed a coup with Carlos Castillo Armas from Honduras. They kicked Jacobo Arbenz out, stripped him naked, humiliated him and he ended up becoming a refugee in Mexico. After that, the U.S. backed up criminal dictatorship after criminal dictatorship in Guatemala in order to benefit the United Fruit Company. How about that? This country was built by laws. Right. It was also built by imperial actions, illegal coups, by Monroe's Manifest Destiny Doctrine, by President James Polk's invention in 1846 of an excuse to wage war against Mexico (the Guadalupe Hidalgo Treaty when the U.S. invaded Mexico and put the American flag up all the way down in Mexico City). In fact, people like Henry David Thoreau, the great writer of "Civil Disobedience," stopped paying taxes because they thought that what the U.S. was doing then was illegal. Abraham Lincoln, who at that time was a young congressman said: Give me proof that there has been blood spilled in our territory. Nope. The land [that the U.S. took from Mexico] was in dispute. The U.S. created a law-breaking atmosphere from the start. And now they come on their high horse saying that they are the great defenders of the law. They invaded Iraq against international law. And was what they did to the Native Americans legal?

PM: Two: Just get in line.

RL: This is also a false argument. There is no line for Mexicans, for instance. You cannot say: I have nothing against immigrants; I'm only against those who come illegally. Historically speaking, you cannot avoid noting, for instance, that during WWII, Braceros (Mexican field workers) came into the U.S. as temporary guest workers in an agreement between both governments. It turns out it was a successful plan. The Braceros changed the agricultural map of the U.S. for the better. The land owners asked the U.S. authorities to prolong the Bracero Program. But what did the U.S. want? They just wanted more "arms" [*Bracero* comes from the Spanish *brazos*, which means arms]. The Braceros were human beings and they started having children. But when the Great Depression came, so did the mass deportations. The U.S. even deported people who'd been born here; the children of those field workers who obviously had erected their lives here. The U.S. constructed a new form of slavery. In the past, they found a way to go kidnap black people from Africa. Now they had found a way for people to come by themselves, fleeing from global economic injustice, which is clearly not controlled by immigrant-exporting nations. Global economic injustice is under control of immigrant-importing nations. Often a powerful country closes its left eye so that undocumented immigrants may come in, but as soon as it wants to criminalize those same immigrants, well, it opens its right eye. There's a double morality and a great hypocrisy. The undocumented immigrant work force substituted the Afro-American servitude in the U.S. After African-Americans became emancipated, undocumented immigrant labor was needed. Starting in 1848, when the Guadalupe Hidalgo Treaty was signed, Mexican labor has subsidized a great amount of the United States' economic development. That is something the U.S. does not want to recognize. They talk about immigration as if it were only a legal matter. It's a way to hide a complex economic reality. It's much easier to get behind a simplistic argument: Illegals, they just come in without getting in line. Sure, sure.

PM: Do people misread the immigration issue due to the system or is there a group of obscure men in suits behind the mess, planning, conspiring?

RL: It's due to a system. But there are also many obscure men from big corporations linked to great interests; namely, oil, agriculture and finances. And now there's a new instrument to extend that power: free trade agreements. Trade is good. Free trade is great. But it turns out that NAFTA (North American Free Trade Agreement) which came into effect on January 1, 1994, has supplementary agreements that took years to take effect, in which U.S. products like beans and corn (corn, imagine that!) now come into Mexico without paying tariffs. And those products are subsidized by the U.S. government. There is no fair competition. It's a legal war which is collapsing the Mexican farm workers' economy. So poor workers first migrate within Mexico to, say, Guadalajara, Monterrey or Mexico City. Then they can't get the basics there either, so where do you think they move to? Guatemala? They migrate to the U.S. because, as Luis Espulto used to say, hunger strikes harder than all.

PM: Three: We love legal Mexicans, just not illegals.

RL: A lot of the people who are now legal U.S. residents were part of a process in which they at some point were undocumented immigrants. There are also those who were crossed by the border. For many, the point in which the concept of Mexican-American was started, took place from one day to the next, in 1848 when the Guadalupe Hidalgo Treaty was signed. Those Mexicans were no longer Mexican, but Mexican-Americans. Many Mexicans stayed in the U.S. [after the Southwest became part of the U.S]. They were given the option to stay. But then the U.S. government, also illegally, changed one of the articles of the Guadalupe Hidalgo Treaty. It didn't respect the rights for Mexicans to, among other things, own land. Then came persecution and a siege. That's the origin of what we are now talking about. Plus, there are no choices for those whom I call economic refugees. And they are economic refugees because of economic policies imposed by the powerful ones: the United States, the International Monetary Fund, the World Bank, all those organizations which are part of this predatory globalization. Sure the U.S wants to welcome [by way of visas] those light-skinned, educated Mexicans who probably graduated from places like Monterrey Tech University, thus reproducing Mexican classism. Those are welcomed, but why? They are young, educated and ready to work. They are ready to get incorporated into U.S. capitalism. Yet those huge, uneducated masses, those without a chance to go to school, are left in Mexico. Well, let poor folks down there kill each other in an eventual civil war!

PM: Four: Illegal aliens do not pay taxes. They merely abuse the system. They go to the hospital and use up resources. They send their children to public schools and use up resources. They walk on the streets and use up the sidewalk. All of this while not paying taxes.

RL: Not true. We can go ask people who do taxes. Evidently, undocumented immigrants get false documents and pay taxes. Immigration lawyers are known to tell undocumented immigrants they should pay taxes so they can get their papers and become citizens in case there is an immigration reform. This is a great myth as far as I know. And in terms of undocumented immigrants using up the resources, well, many don't use the resources because they're afraid of being deported.

PM: Five: Mexicans shouldn't complain. Mexico mistreats Central Americans way worse than the U.S. mistreats Mexicans.

RL: Totally true, but it's not Mexico who mistreats Central Americans, but the hypocritical Mexican government. Also, we should not forget that Mexico has agreements with the U.S. There is an unsigned treaty besides NAFTA that took place in 2005 in Waco, Texas, called SPP (Security and Prosperity Partnership of North America) where all those immigration themes were addressed. In a way, Mexico does the dirty work for the U.S. They stop Central American immigration half way through. Mexico is serving the U.S. as a kind of border patrol.

PM: So you think the U.S. prompts the Mexican abuse

of Central American immigrants in Mexico.

RL: In general, the U.S. encourages what is happening. It wants to stop these hordes of people coming from Central America by way of treaties. They put pressure on Mexico so it stops Central Americans in Mexico. But forget about the terrible institutional approach for a minute. Many there rape women and young men and give them horrendous beatings. Coming through Mexico is a deadly painful customs patrol; evidently, a criminal one as well. The Mexican government cannot overlook this and then complain about what the U.S. does to Mexican immigrants. But Mexico overlooks this because they have to do it. They are at the U.S. government's mercy. I want you to put this down: I'm not just blaming this problem on the United States. Mexican administrations that have not built the conditions for a clean, fair, employed Mexico, which does not bend over backwards to undignified international demands. are also to blame. Above all, I give responsibility to our [Latin American] governments. Though, at the same time, they are punished by the U.S if they don't do what they are told. Bilateral blame, that's what we have here.

PM: Six: Let's close the borders first. Then we can decide what to do with the folks who already live here.

RL: In the end, that's dealing with the effects of the problem and not with the causes. Are you a dad?

PM: No.

RL: When you have a sick child who gets a fever at 3

a.m. and you call the doctor and the doctor does not pick up the phone and you want to deal with the fever, well, you give your child something, anything, to lower the fever. But what if the child has an infection? You are not dealing with the infection by lowering the fever. It's just the same. You can send the National Guard to the border. You can send whoever you want. That is just going to be a temporary palliative treatment to get the fever down. It's not going to solve the problem. You need to deal with the infection. The infection here is an unjust global economy and badly drafted free trade agreements that benefit big corporations, not society.

PM: Seven: Terrorists might enter the U.S. through the Mexican border.

RL: According to the official 9/11 conspiracy theory, these men came in through Canada. Now, they could have come in any other way, but they came in through Canada. It's true that they could come through the southern border. There needs to be an agreement [with Mexico] as with any other country in the world. But terrorists could enter by plane or they could well be here already. Many have come in with student visas, or whatever. This means they've come in legally. Not illegally. Another great myth.

PM: Eight: The SB 1070 Arizona law is doing nothing more than helping execute the federal law.

RL: In a sense, they are right in arguing that they are executing the federal law's spirit. But they are also trying to politically manipulate this problem which has economic, sociological and political implications. It's not only about implementing a law. The problems immigration carries with it for the federal government must be understood in terms of internal and foreign relations and treaties. The federal government takes in mind internal and external consequences that a local approach cannot even begin to understand. Evidently, the SB 1070 is not constitutional. That's true. But I think that is the weakest argument against it. There are stronger arguments against this law. And they have to do with America's responsibility, or co-responsibility, at the problem's root. It has to do with how the U.S. government has caused the illegal immigration problem by way of its foreign policy.

PM: Ten: When one goes into a club, security guards ask you for your ID card to make sure you're old enough to enter. This is the same as the police potentially checking for people's residency papers. No big deal.

RL: The thing is, little by little, we can get closer to George Orwell's "1984" world. We could get there fast with a million excuses, such as fear and security. I come back to the same thing: Let's make a world with a human face.

A Cocaine Moratorium

Two men stand side by side in front of the only urinal inside a bar's restroom in Chinatown. Both look up, a little scared, as I open the door. I apologize realizing they must have forgotten to lock the door.

One of them speaks before I leave. "We're just doing some lines," he says, his fear turning into a mischievous smile.

"That's alright," I say, jokingly. "The '80s are back."

They laugh and dust off their noses in front of the mirror before heading back out. I don't really think anything of the matter as I relieve myself of about a gallon of Tsingtao. It's a bar in Los Angeles. What's there to think about?

I might have not been thinking about it, but some people were.

A good year later, I get together for lunch in Koreatown with Liz, a friend who's a lawyer. Our conversation revolves, as it invariably seems to do nowadays for people in my generation, around the subject of money troubles and looming old age. We're getting pretty damned close to 30. Everything has changed or is about to change for us.

"I now work in an office, stay home cleaning up during my free time, and don't even do drugs anymore. I don't even know if I want to do them," she says. "I wouldn't want to contribute to all the shit that's going down in Mexico right now, you know?"

Her words get me thinking.

Here's the thing. I'm not into drugs because I'm not really interested and even if I were interested, I feel like my mind isn't strong enough. I could relate a handful of bad experiences here, but this isn't the place. Let's just say that personally, I just say no, but to say that I'm against drugs would be an overstatement. I'm all about giving people the freedom to choose what they put in their bodies, even if it's to their own detriment.

Not that drugs are always bad. Like the late comedic giant Bill Hicks, I think that the positive aspects of occasional drug use are curiously taboo. Hicks said that drugs can make people more spiritual by showing them that life is nothing but a dream, a different dimension, or something like that. That's too Lizard King for me. But I agree with the fact that a little drug consumption could loosen a person up and even make that person more creative. I guess I wouldn't trust somebody who hasn't smoked pot at least once. Though, at the same time, I wouldn't trust somebody who, as the song goes, smokes two joints in the morning and smokes two joints at night. That's too much.

But this isn't about pot. It's about cocaine. Marijuana might be the most widely produced drug in the world, but it's also mostly trafficked within countries and does not produce near the amount of death and violence cocaine does. Cocaine, the second most produced drug in the world, on the other hand, causes a great amount of violence. According to the 2011 United Nations World Drug Report, cocaine is "probably the most problematic drug in terms of trafficking-related violence."

Liz' words echo in my mind. "I wouldn't want to contribute to all the shit that's going down in Mexico right now, you know?"

I know. Not long ago, if somebody told me that he or she was an occasional cocaine user, I wouldn't have thought less of that person. I mean, even my favorite literary detective, Sherlock Holmes, was a bit of a cokehead. But I've kind of changed my mind, which has messed me up. Maybe I'm just afraid of turning into a self-righteous old man. Being open minded, going with the flow, looking the other way, not minding if you don't mind, having all kinds of friends: that's how I've always lived my life. I've never been the "Just Say No" type. In fact, I've always hated the "Just Say No" types.

And yet now I feel I have to take a stand as a politically minded Latin American. I hate grand statements like that, but the situation in Mexico is just too awful for ambivalence, so here it is. At this point in American history, doing drugs —particularly cocaine and its derivatives— even occasionally strikes me as an altogether unethical action. Official Mexican government figures state that more than (much more, according to unofficial figures) 34,000 people have died in drug-related violence since December 2006, when former Mexican President Felipe Calderón launched an all-out war against drug cartels. Over 15,000 people died last year alone.

If numbers do nothing for you, please close your

eyes for a minute and visualize a field full of decapitated bodies. That's what drugs —particularly cocaine, which has a huge share of the drug market— are doing to Mexico on a daily basis. There's no shedding the American part of the blame. According to the United Nations, about 41 percent of cocaine used in the world is consumed in North America (36 percent in the United States).

What would I have done differently in that Chinatown bathroom a year ago now that I've made up my mind about cocaine? Not much. I wouldn't have joked about it (actually, yes I would have). I'm still not the kind of person that can tell strangers what to do. At least not in person. In writing, well, that's a different deal: just say no, kiddos. This is not about freedom. It's about the lives of others

World Bloggers and the New Democracy Struggle

Before the advent of internet self-publishing at the end of the 20th century, world dictators were able to subdue rebellious publishing ventures by, for instance, physically closing down printing presses. Back then publishing was easier to control because widespread distribution of written materials was centralized. That is no longer the case. Self-publishing tools, particularly blogs, have decentralized the ability to publish dissent anywhere. That said, the old perils for those willing to publish thoughts against dictatorial regimes (persecution, incarceration, torture and death) have not gone away.

During a' 2011 speech at George Washington University, "Internet Rights and Wrongs," Hillary Clinton celebrated this major communications' shift by comparing social media to public squares. She was careful, however, to note that a repressive backlash is already taking place.

"In China, the government censors content and redirects search results to error pages. In Burma, independent news sites have been taken down with distributed denial of service attacks. In Cuba, the government is trying to create a national intranet, while not allowing their citizens to access the global internet. In Vietnam, bloggers who criticize the government are arrested and abused. In Iran, the authorities block opposition and media websites, target social media, and steal identifying information about their own people to hunt them down."

Why, then, didn't most dictatorships stop blogging and other social media technologies as soon as they appeared? The speed with which those tools rose to prominence is a major part of the answer. Blogging, for instance, became influential in just three years.

In January 1999, San Francisco-based internet entrepreneurs Evan Williams and Meg Hourihan co-founded Pyra Labs, a tiny software creation company. They had many ideas and did not know how to make them available to each other online. To solve the problem they created a little website where text could be posted, dated and saved. They called it Blogger and it was a hit. As Scott Rosenberg reports in his book *Say Everything,* by 2002, around 70,000 Blogger accounts had been created. Google bought up the company in February 2003 and membership increased to millions. By the 2004 American presidential elections, political blogging had already become a factor.

Many dissidents living in dictatorships also started blogging. This essay is about them: the first generation of dissident world bloggers. Ai Weiwei from China, Hossein Derakhshan from Iran and Yoani Sánchez from Cuba are three of the most influential pro-democracy blogging pioneers of the 2000s. These three brave democracy activists represent a whole movement. Their individual struggles illustrate common features of the new war between writers and dictators in the wake of global access to cheap self-publishing tools.

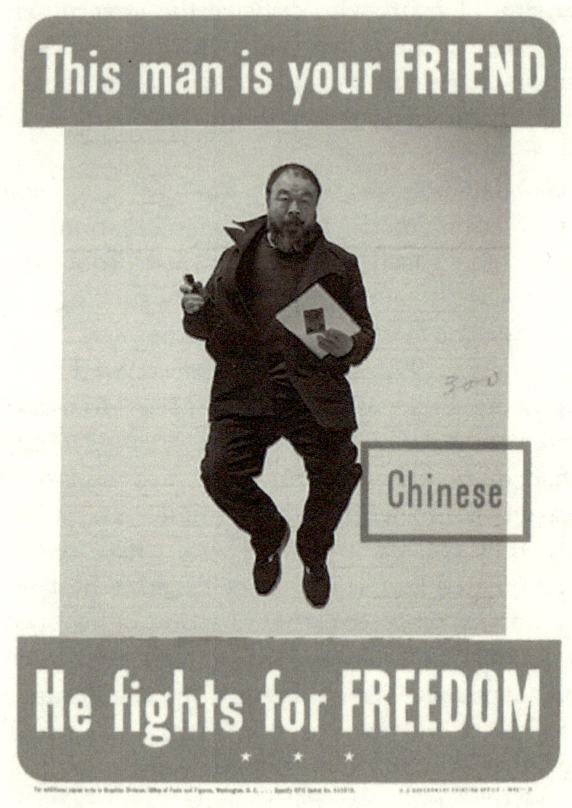

Images by Mia Chamasmany

Ai Weiwei, China

The night before the trial, the most famous Chinese artist in the world, Ai Weiwei, checked into a Chengdu hotel. At around 3 a.m. a group of policemen knocked on his room's door. When he refused to open it, they broke in.

Ai had traveled from Beijing to Chengdu, Sichuan province, to testify in Tan Zuoren's August 12, 2009 trial. He apparently knew things that could help exonerate Tan, a fellow blogger who had set up an independent list of victims in relation to May 2008's Sichuan earthquake. Coincidentally, Ai was working on a victim's list of his own.

A year had passed since the earthquake, which killed around 70,000 people, had devastated Sichuan province. Like Tan, Ai Weiwei believed that Chinese authorities were not publishing an official victim's list in order to hide their own corruption. Both men also believed that so many of the earthquake's victims were children because several collapsed schools (colloquially called tofu-dregs) had been built using cheap materials and ignoring safety regulations. An independent victim's list could clarify matters.

Due to his many controversial dealings with the Chinese state, Ai is given to recording all of his interactions with authorities. So right before the police broke into his hotel room, he turned on a small audio recording device. The scuffle can be heard in *Disturbing the Peace* (2009) and *So Sorry* (2012), two documentary films Ai made using that night's audio.

"Who hit you? Where? Where is the wound?" asks a policeman, after another policeman apparently assaulted Ai in the dark.

"How did my clothes get torn?" Ai asks.

"You did it yourself," says the policeman.

"I tore off my own clothes and beat myself?"

"Right."

That able adults should argue about an event that has just taken place seems odd. It isn't. It just is an unequivocal symptom of dictatorship. In China, as in most other dictatorships, as soon as a significant event happens, a *truth versus lies* battle ignites. This happens because, as George Orwell put it in "On the Prevention of Literature," his classic 1946 essay, "Totalitarianism demands, in fact, the continuous alteration of the past, and in the long run probably demands a disbelief in the very existence of objective truth." In most dictatorships, a citizen can either accept the official version of the truth or he can fight to establish what he thinks is true. The latter is a critical political action.

The battle of Tan Zuoren's trial was won by the Chinese state. Ai was kept from attending and Tan got five years in prison. The sentence was "inciting subversion from state power."

There were also the physical consequences of the beating. When Ai went back home to Beijing, he started getting headaches and found it difficult to concentrate. After that, about a month went by. Ai flew to Munich to set up a major solo exhibition, "So Sorry," at the Haus der Kunst Museum. In Munich, the pain and dizziness became acute, so he had to be rushed to a hospital. The doctors found pooled blood around his brain. They opened two small holes in his skull to drain it out. Blood was putting pressure on his brain. The hotel beating was the cause. Had the German doctors not made the openings in his skull, Ai could have gone into a coma or died.

Political repression is nothing new to Ai. The year he was born, 1957, his father, Ai Qing, a celebrated Chinese poet, was accused of being a rightist. True or not, such an accusation in the late '50s (a time when the Chinese regime was cleaning up so-called bourgeois sprouts within its intelligentsia by way of the Anti-

Rightist Movement) could be devastating. Ai's family had to leave their home in Beijing so that the father could be "ideologically rehabilitated." The accusation resulted in Ai Weiwei spending his formative years in a wandering, politically punitive mode. Some of the places where the family was forced to live were a lumberjack's home in the Dongbei Forest, Soviet-style block housing, and even an earthen pit.

Of all those places, the pit seems to have had the greatest impact on him. In "Here and Now" (2006), a blog entry published in the book *Ai Weiwei's Blog*, he described it as a "ditch dug into the ground, and covered with branches and mud." In another entry published that same month, "Ideal Cities and Architecture Do Not Exist," he linked his preference for "common sense" as opposed to "ideal" architecture to the ditch's flexibility as a living space. "Because we were a family of readers, we needed a bookshelf in our home," he wrote."My father dug out a hole; in my opinion, that was the best bookshelf."

That the artist who helped design China's flagship 21st century building, the Bird's Nest Stadium, for the country's capitalistic coming-out party (the 2008 Olympics) was forced to spend part of his childhood in a hole, which was later turned into a pigpen, is one of those extravagant ironies abundant in most dictatorships.

In 1976, the family got lucky. Mao died, the Gang of Four were arrested, the Cultural Revolution ended, the regime's policies became more liberal and they were allowed to go back home. About twenty years had passed since the Ai's had been forced to leave Beijing. By the time they were allowed to return, however, Ai Weiwei had grown up. In 1978, he enrolled in the

Beijing Film Academy, and in 1981, he was able to move to New York City, where he lived for about a decade. In New York, he attended art school, took photos, and got his first art shows. Still, despite the dictatorship, he moved back to China.

It was 1993 and he was in his mid-thirties. He immersed himself in Beijing's East Village, an influential group of radical artists that gathered around Beijing's Eastern outskirts. In the mid-'90s he published the seminal *Black, White and Gray Cover Books*, an anthology of the group's work, which he saw as the first pieces of original Chinese modern art ever made. After that, his artistic work took off.

In 2006, he started blogging to massive success. In fact, he became known to more people in China due to his blog than due to to his art. While his blog was active, he took apart China's zeitgeist and came to disturbing conclusions: China is still deeply repressed, China is lost, China is spiritually sick, and, most importantly, the Chinese regime is lying to its people and the Chinese people are lying to themselves. He blogged about all kinds of things, yet everything linked back to political repression. Even his writing style seemed political. He never took anything for granted. It's as if he inspected every thought for ideological pollution before using it.

He defined all that came his way. In "On Photography," (2006) he defined reality: "The universe's reality is limited and ruthless; humankind's reality is comparatively psychological and emotional, indeterminate, difficult to ponder, idealistic, and self-centered." In "Ordinary Architecture," (2006) he defined himself: "for me, solving problems has always been the most important, most basic characteristic of my personality."

In "Chinese Contemporary Art in Dilemma and Transition" (2006) he tried defining China: "Economically speaking, a system on the verge of extinction remade itself as a materialist society." And, in that same entry, he attempted perhaps the most difficult definition of all: China's character. "Metaphor, ambiguity, manifold significance, illusion and the willingness to deliberately confound right and wrong have always been signature expressions of Chinese culture and particular modes of thought and speech within this ancient Eastern country."

2008, the year of the earthquake, marks a turn for the negative in Ai's outlook. In "We Have Nothing" (2008), he gives one of his most ruthless diagnoses of China: "A country that rejects truth, refuses to change and lacks a spirit of freedom is hopeless." He said he did not even consider China a modern country because modernity cannot exist without freedom of speech. And yet, Ai's anger was directed not only at the state, but at his fellow countrymen, who, he argued, lack the spirit and creativity to fight for freedom. In "Karmic Retribution for Karma" (2008) he wrote, "I've realized the vengeance that is the absence of Karmic retribution and thus China's survival is her most genuine form of punishment." By the end of the year, disappointment reached a personal level. In "Bullshit is Free" (2008), he said, "It's so pathetic that we should have to fight for things so basic that I can barely find reason to continue on this way."

If the immediate source of Ai's frustration could be put in one sentence, it would come from that same entry: "Thousands of children perished in one instant as a result of tofu-dregs engineering, and yet people sit in front of their televisions like wooden chickens."

Soon he acted beyond the scopes of the blog. In July 2008, asked the following three questions about the tragedy: 1) How many people were actually killed and wounded in the Wenchuan earthquake? 2) How did they perish, and who should shoulder the blame? 3) Exactly how many students died as a result of these tofu-dreg schools?

Those weren't rhetorical questions. Ai was out to find out. Years earlier he had stated in his blog that problem-solving was the most basic quality of his personality. So, March 20, 2009, close to a year after the Wenchuan earthquake, Ai and a group of about a hundred volunteers began the Citizen Investigation. As editor and translator Lee Ambrozy reported on Ai Weiwei's blog, Ai and the volunteers went to earthquake zones, interviewed people and put pressure on officials to reveal the number of victims. He collected more than 5,000 names of dead children before authorities shut down his blog May 28, 2009. According to Ambrozy, around that same time police tapped Ai's phone, intercepted his text messages, and put two surveillance cameras outside his home.

Almost three years have transpired this way. In early 2011, his new Shanghai studio was demolished for his supposed failure to comply with building regulations. That same year, he was arrested for 81 days for "tax evasion." The conditions in which he was kept were harsh, bordering on torture. He reportedly lost 28 pounds. After paying a $1.3 million bail, much of which came from donations, he was released, but is now on probation. He cannot leave Beijing without official permission.

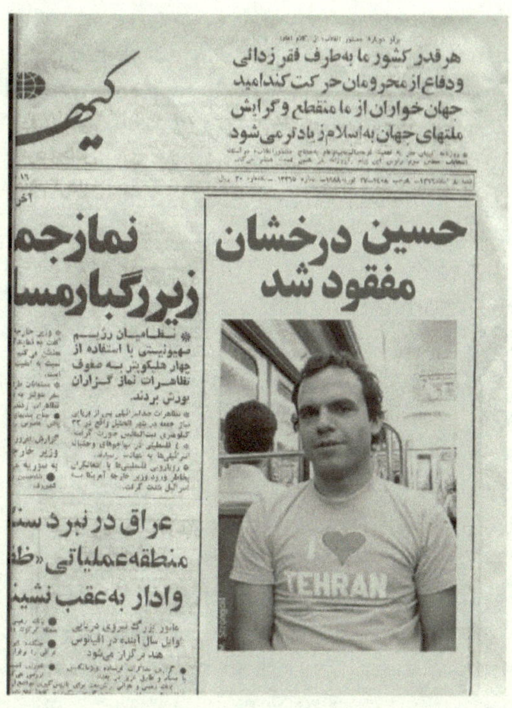

کیهان

هر قدر کشور ما به‌طرف فقر زدائی
ودفاع از محرومان حرکت کند امید
جهان‌خواران از ما منقطع و گرایش
ملتهای جهان به اسلام زیادتر می‌شود

نمازجم...
زیر رگبار مسا...

نظامیان رژیم صهیونیستی با استفاده از چهار هلیکوپتر به صفوف تظاهرات نماز گزاران یورش بردند.

حسین درخشان
مفقود شد

عراق در نبرد سن...
منطقه‌عملیاتی «ظ...
وادار به‌عقب نشین...

مانور بزرگ نیروی دریایی اوایل سال آینده در اقیانوس هند برگزار می‌شود

Hossein Derakhshan, Iran

Neighboring countries like Afghanistan and Saudi Arabia are behind Iran in terms of internet access. This is because Iranian leaders invested on the internet early on. The investment's goal was to achieve economic growth, not to create social reform outlets, but back in the early '90s the Iranian autocratic government was probably not fully aware of the internet's socially progressive possibilities. By now it probably knows better.

In 2009, Iran saw a wave of protests that threatened the country's theocratic regime. Social media played a huge role in those protests. In fact, some called it the Twitter Revolution. It's easy to imagine the Iranian autocrats wishing their country's internet surge had never taken place. But that surge wasn't easy to destroy. It has been going on for over twenty years.

Iran first went online in 1992. Three years later, there were 30,000 internet users. Many high-tech investments followed. The 1997 election of a relatively liberal president, Mohammad Khatami, helped. In the book *The Internet of Elsewhere*, Cyrus Farivar reports that in 2005, at the end of the Khatami administration, an eleven-year, $700 million internet infrastructure project was completed. "Today," he writes, "Iran has the fastest growth rate of internet users of any Middle Eastern country." It went from 1 million Internet users in 2005 to 23 million in 2008. Now more than a third of Iran's 79 million citizens are online. Consider the fact that 70 percent of Iranians are under 30 years of age and that the country has an 85 percent literacy rate, and the Iranian regime's problem becomes apparent. Web-linked middle classes are reform minded.

Hossein Derakhshan, one of Iran's blogging pioneers, was born in Tehran in 1975. Around 1999, he was a young technology journalist in that same city, but the government closed down the paper he worked for. By the end of 2000 he moved to Toronto. In September of the following year, he opened a blog and called it Editor: Myself. Yet, blogging in Persian was complicated because most websites only worked with Latin-alphabet-based languages. A program named Unicode made it possible for applications to read other languages, but most people did not know how to use it.

In late 2000, Derakhshan solved the problem. He wrote up a step-by-step guide on how to post in Persian using Unicode and Pyra Lab's new application, Blogger.

Derakhshan's guide was nothing short of foundational. Blogging in Iran took off. In fact, Iranian bloggers began affectionately calling him "The Blogfather."

Hossein Derakhshan's contributions as a political critic, however, aren't as clear as his technical contributions. In his blog, hoder.com, and columns for The Guardian and The Washington Post, he showed a puzzling ambivalence about many important issues. Adjectives like "relatively" abound in Derakhshan's writing. In his eyes, most events in Iran during the first decade of the 21st century were *relatively* free, *relatively* reliable, *relatively* independent, and, of course, *relatively* democratic. This is quite different, for instance, from Ai Weiwei's writing, which is loaded with livid, at times vulgar, denunciations of the Chinese political apparatus.

In "No Iranian Che," (2005), written after Mahmoud Ahmadinejad, a conservative, was elected president, Derakhshan argued that Ayatollah Ali Khameni, Iran's theocratic leader, allowed "a relatively democratic election to take place." The term "relatively" seemed confusing. It went against the Iranian authorities, who claimed the elections were fully democratic, but also against the West, which tends to see countries as democratic or dictatorial, not something in between.

And yet, Derakhshan's writing wasn't supportive of his country's dictatorship. Quite the opposite. In "Why Iran loves Zidane," (2006), a column about the Soccer World Cup, he took apart Ahmadinejad. "He is not a fundamentalist, he is a populist," he said. The distinction is important for someone like Derakhshan, who believed Iran's government should change for the better, but not all at once. He never said, nor implied, as expected from a dissident blogger, that his country's system was an authoritarian theocracy that had to be replaced at any cost. Because of this, many exiled Iranians called Derakhshan a sellout. Accusations against him were all over the internet.

Calling the blogfather a sellout was a reasonable assertion. It sure looked that way. But it was incorrect.

Some of Derakhshan's journalistic actions for Editor: Myself were confrontational. In January 2006, he visited Israel as a peace-seeking blogger (he was a Canadian citizen at this point). He said his goal was to "show the Israelis that the vast majority of Iranians do not identify with Ahmadinejad's rhetoric, despite what it looks like from the outside." He also wanted to explain to the people of Israel "how any kind of violent action against Iran would only harm the young people who are gradually reforming the system and how the radicals would benefit from such situation." The second part of his plan was to show "the real Israel" to his 20,000 Iranian readers.

Visiting Israel is against the law in Iran. Tehran sees Jerusalem as the enemy. Like many of the most respected bloggers from isolated regimes, Derakhshan's bold actions turned him into a liaison between antagonistic countries, a sort of unofficial diplomat. The Israeli media covered his visit. The problem was that Derakhshan's conciliatory plan put him in direct confrontation with Iran's dictatorship. By publicly traveling to Israel, he had crossed the speech-only line. Now he could really become a target of the Iranian regime.

And yet, as confrontational as his actions had

become, Derakhshan could still not be called a particularly progressive political thinker. In fact, once back in Toronto from Israel, he penned a rather shocking column, "Iran Needs Nuclear Weapons," (2006). He thought that no matter how democratic Iran were to become, the United States would still try to put in a puppet government it could control. "For this reason," he said, "I believe Iran needs to produce nuclear weapons as a defensive mechanism, to deter the U.S. today and the ever-expanding and equally energy-hungry China tomorrow." Then, in a column titled "Stop Bullying Iran" (2007), he took it a bit further. In an unusually emotive tone, he said that if the United States were to wage war against Iran he "would absolutely go back and defend Iran." He prefaced this claim by calling the Islamic Republic "a valuable cause worth defending," and one that even "at its worst, is way better than anything that the United States or anyone else can bring to Iran."

Probably guessing that his exiled Iranian readers might react against his views, he then defined himself. "I'm not saying this as a fervent religious man with sexy Ahmadinejad's posters on my wall. In fact, I am an atheist and this can easily get me into serious trouble in any Islamic country... And of course I do have the dream of an open, free, fair and secular Iran run by competent and representative officials." For some people that self-definition wasn't enough. In some Iranian expat circles, Hossein Derakhshan, the man who had made it possible for people to blog in Persian, the Blogfather, had lost his dissident status. Or to put it another way, he had managed to antagonize everyone: the Iranian regime, the United States, and even other fellow dissident bloggers.

Perhaps he thought going pro-nuclear would win him the Islamic Republic's love or ameliorate its resentment towards him when he went back. If that's what he thought, he was dead wrong. On November 1, 2008, while back in Tehran, authorities arrested him at his parents' home. Given the distance from the West, and the Iranian authorities' secrecy, his situation became hard to follow. Some newspapers said the Iranian regime was accusing Derakhshan of spying for Israel. Different media outlets had different theories. Close to a year went by. Not even his parents in Iran were sure about what their son was being accused of. They didn't even know where he was detained.

In October 2009, his father, Hassan Derakhshan, wrote a letter to Ayatollah Amoli Larijani, head of the Department of the Judiciary, asking for information.

"Please imagine that for every six months we just saw him for very few minutes. We have no information about his legal situation. No court has been held yet and we don't know which institution or security organization Hossein is under the control of. "

Later that month, Derakhshan's parents were allowed to visit Derakhshan in Tehran's Evin Prison. During the visit he reportedly confirmed that he'd been beat up and forced to do squats in cold showers. There were also reports by the group Human Rights Activists in Iran stating Derakhshan "spent the first eight months of his detention in solitary confinement..." and was pressured to testify against himself. Moreover, it had been over a year after being arrested, but he had still not been legally charged with anything.

Derakhshan's trial finally began on June 23, 2010, over a year and a half after he'd been taken into custody. It took place at the Tehran Revolutionary

Court. There prosecutors requested he be sentenced to death. Those requests did not proceed. On September 28, he was sentenced to 19 and a half years in prison. The reason? Among other charges, co-operating with enemy states, managing obscene websites, and insulting religious leaders.

Ironically, in a 2007 piece titled "Cut the Bias," Derakhshan had written that "Iran doesn't have a policy of imprisoning people for the content of their blogs as some human rights campaigners would have us believe." He attacked Western organizations such as Reporters Without Borders for making too much of Iran's repressive policy towards its bloggers, particularly those with little readership. He said that many groups "rush into demonizing a government that they are already against and don't care much to cover the further developments, especially if they are positive." Little did he know that about a year and a half later, he would be imprisoned for his postings and that groups like Reporters Without Borders would try to help him get free.

Ideologically antagonizing everyone, however, should not be punishable by law. The ideas someone publishes aren't the problem. As Orwell put it in "The Prevention of Literature," "What is really at issue is the right to report contemporary events truthfully, or as truthfully as is consistent with the ignorance, bias and self-deception from which every observer necessarily suffers." In other words, whatever Derakhshan wrote, he was trying to make sense of a vexing situation *in real time.* That alone puts him on the side of democracy, which is why he ended up in jail.

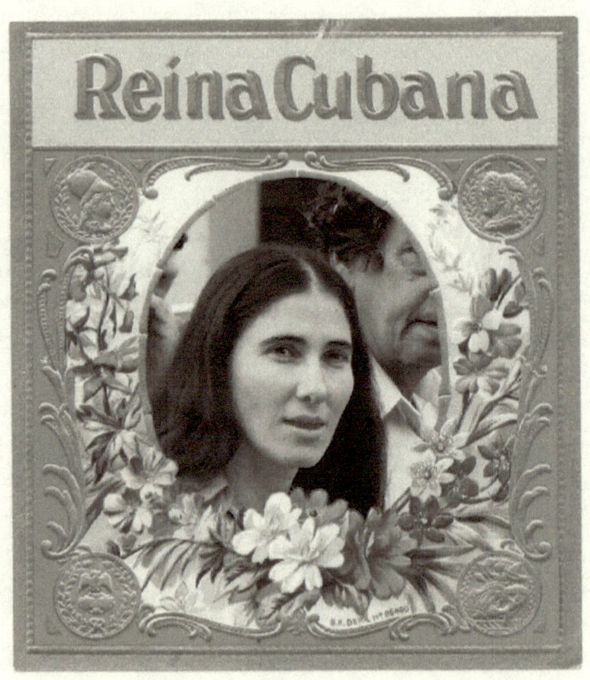

Yoani Sánchez, Cuba

In 2002, Yoani Sánchez managed to flee Cuba for Switzerland. She was under 30, had a degree in Philology and could have begun a new life. Yet two years later, she moved back to her dictatorship-ravaged country. It is unclear why ("family reasons," she wrote in her blog). What is clear is that before going back, she gave herself two challenges: to live within Cuba as a free person would and to face the consequences of that decision. Like Derakhshan, who moved back to Iran from Canada fully aware that he could get arrested, and Ai Weiwei, who moved back to China after living in the States for over a decade, Sánchez's decision seemed to defy common sense.

It was also defiant of the regime. In April 2007, six months after buying a laptop from a rafter who needed money for an engine (a rafter is a person who tries to flee Cuba by way of a home-made boat), she started her blog, Generación Y. She was inspired to blog after reading blog postings by a Cuban Communist Party member. Unlike the communist blogger, who used the internet to denounce people trading goods on the black market, Sánchez's purpose was to keep her sanity. "The scene is simple: A weak woman, without dreams, sits down to describe what is not reflected on the boring TV or in the tedious national newspaper," she wrote in the prologue to *Havana Real*, a translated book anthologizing her best posts from 2007 to 2010.

Though Sánchez is less nuanced than Derakhshan and not as deeply analytical as Ai, her blog comes across as the most sincere of the three. In fact, her posts are close to testimony, even evidence. She most often reports at the hyper-local and personal levels. Individual hunger, lust, resentment and filth get as much or more attention in her blog as do political events. When she does talk about political events, they are always linked to their effects on actual people, many of whom she knows. Her detailed descriptions of hunger and human secretions serve another purpose: they fight the quasi-religious dictatorial rhetoric. Instead of bearded titans battling empires while erecting radical new social orders, which is the Cuban regime's narrative, her postings are peopled by average, underfed folks like herself, who roam the island in search of a piece of chicken to cook for dinner or some toilet paper to wipe their behinds.

"She and her daughters cut up a couple of sheets and managed to make some pads, which they washed after each use," Sánchez wrote in "Trivialities," (2009). The posting tells the story of Xiomara, a woman from a town where sanitary pads have not come for four months and who must use extreme ingenuity when her period comes.

Generación Y is full of such in-your-face accounts. It presents a plethora of detailed looks at people's intimate problems. Sánchez's sharply focused posts are like small pictures in a photo mosaic. They delineate a complex system of hunger, persecution, chaos and bullshit—in short, dictatorship.

The following paragraph is made up of fragments taken from separate posts written between 2007 and 2010 as collected in *Havana Real.*

The effect is cinematic:

"I challenge you to find a public clock in this city [Havana] that tells the time or at least an approximation of the real time." "An egg now costs four Cuban pesos, one-third the average wage for a day's labor." "When I see myself reduced to fighting for food, I feel bad and prefer to come home with an empty shopping bag." "To mark the country's fifty-year anniversary on January 1, we were allowed to buy a half a pound of ground beef through the ration system." "None of the children knows the sensation of a jet of water falling on shoulders." "How do you shout on Twitter?" "How will I look at him and tell him his mother has been beaten up on a public street for writing a blog?" "The

State has been looted by the State itself." "My mother called me early to tell me there is toilet paper at a distant market." "On the corner is a hydrant that is the only water supply for hundreds of families in the area." "These public cameras —the embodiment of the Orwellian 'telescreen'— have ushered in a new form of cinema."

During her over five years as a blogger, Sánchez has neatly executed her original truth-telling plan. And it has paid off. Blogging has turned what she at first self-deprecatingly called a "weak woman, without dreams" into the best known dissident blogger in the world. In 2008, one of Spain's most important newspapers, El País, awarded her an Ortega y Gasset online journalism award. The following year she was the first blogger to be given Columbia University's prestigious Maria Moors Cabot journalism award. She's also the only blogger to have interviewed American president Barack Obama.

But the regime's retaliation has been tough. In June 2008, Fidel Castro, alluded to Sánchez in a prologue to a book titled "Fidel, Bolivia y Algo Más" (Fidel, Bolivia, and More). Castro didn't so much mind the negative things Sánchez allegedly told a Mexican news agency about life Cuba, but *how* people like her are told to generalize the Cuban condition. What he minded the most was that "there exist young Cubans who think like that and serve as special envoys to do dirty work and neocolonial press for the old Spanish metropolis that awards them." That's a bit scary. In Cuba, if Castro isn't fond of you, you might come across trouble. Her situation is particularly critical because Castro stated that he considers her a foreign agent bent on destroying the state.

When a regime comes to such farfetched conclusions it is because it has lost touch with reality. The craziness shows in the state's language. As in Ai Weiwei's case, language dissection has been central to Sánchez writing. It always is for those fighting dictatorships because, as Orwell said in "Politics and the English Language," "to think clearly is a necessary first step towards political regeneration."

In "Similes, Eternity and Power," (2007) Sánchez took issue with a badly constructed simile she often heard in political speeches: "Its fire will be eternal as the Revolution." To dissect it, she went to the dictionary. "It turns out that 'eternal' is not only that which lasts into the future *ad infinitum*, but that which has no beginning, which was always there," she wrote. The idea is that although the Cuban Revolution is a reality today, there obviously was a time when it wasn't one. "Why then this absurd parallelism," she asked "this demonstrably false simile, comparing two transient things —fire and the revolution— claiming that each carries within it the seed of immortality?" By taking apart official language, Sánchez challenged the regime, of course, but also seemed to ease her own dictatorship-island claustrophobia. (Cuban poet Virgilio Piñera's verse, "The curse of being completely surrounded by water," comes to mind). One can almost hear her sigh after the post's last few words. "It's a relief that all the things in this world's days are numbered."

Besides keeping her from traveling for years (eventually, she did travel) making internet access difficult, blocking access to her blog, and banning her books within Cuba, there has also been violence.

On November 6, 2009, Yoani Sánchez and three friends, including writer Orlando Luis Pardo Lazo, were on their way to a peace march in Havana. As Sánchez reported in a post titled "A Gangland-Style Kidnapping" (2009), a black car pulled up near them and three strong strangers came out. One of the strangers grabbed Sánchez's wrist, while the other two surrounded her friends.

"The 'aggressors' called for a patrol car to take two of my companions while Orlando and I were forced into the car," she wrote.

When she called out for help, the attackers apparently threatened bystanders in a peculiar way.

"Don't mess with it, these are counter-revolutionaries!"

No one dared to help them.

The worst part of the assault took place inside the car.

"One man put his knee in my chest and the other, reaching back from the front seat, hit me in the kidneys and then punched me in the head...."

At one point, Sánchez was able to grab one of the aggressor's testicles and dig her nails in, but when she tried to open the door and jump out, she noticed that there was no door handle inside the car, like in a gangster movie.

After the beating, Sánchez and Orlando were dropped off at a different location.

"We cried in each other's arms in the middle of the sidewalk," she wrote.

To think they were walking to a peace march.

Sánchez's decision to move back to Cuba after having been able to escape to a Western democracy might still seem reckless (particularly since at the time she had a young child). But if one looks at the central role she has played in her country's democracy struggle, it becomes clear that moving back was not only reckless; it was also heroic. The same holds true for Ai Weiwei and Hossein Derakhshan, who, driven by curiosity and conviction, went back to their countries without protection from a news agency.

Favorable Times?

In his seminal pamphlet "From Dictatorship to Democracy," Gene Sharp described how dictatorships usually affect citizens.

"The population has often been atomized (turned into a mass of isolated individuals) unable to work together to achieve freedom, to confide in each other, or even to do much of anything at their own initiative. The result is predictable: the population becomes weak, lacks self-confidence, and is incapable of resistance. People are too often frightened to share their hatred of dictatorship and their hunger for freedom even with family and friends. People are often too terrified to think seriously of public resistance."

Sharp's pamphlet was published in 1993, before the rise of internet self-publishing and social media. Matters changed radically within a few years. A key date is Google's February 16, 2003 announcement of its Blogger acquisition. It was the date blogs became a mainstream tool. Another key date is the November 19, 2009 posting of Yoani Sánchez's e-mail interview with Barack Obama. It was the first time an American president gave an interview to a blogger and, most importantly, the political world's official acceptance that dissident bloggers had become players in international politics.

Because of technology, the dreaded politically atomized citizen of the past is now on his way out. As shown by Ai Weiwei, Hossein Derakhshan and Yoani Sánchez, who were all born into dictatorships, most people with an internet connection can now jointly fight autocrats. There are still consequences, of course. Ruthless dictatorial censure and violence abound. And yet as much as the advent of universal political freedom remains a far off vision, most of the evidence points in the same direction. These are favorable times for the pursuit of global democracy.

SELF

Someone Else's Blood

Julio and I ran over a beautiful white cat tonight on Bronson Avenue. We were driving to Cedars-Sinai to see Alejandra, who had just been through a blood transfusion because of her strange anemia. I was speeding, but I'm always speeding. Julio didn't see the cat coming; I did, but couldn't stop in time. The cat was fat and furry and could not cross the street fast enough. And it was just too dark. Some nights are just too fucking dark to see small animals. Anyway, we ran it over and didn't know how to deal with it.

Here's how it happened.

I park the Nissan and look around, but there is nobody around. We want to at least pick it up so other cars don't tear it apart, but neither Julio nor I can do it. He says that the blood could be infectious or that the cat could still be alive and it could turn around and bite us and scratch us. I don't say anything. I don't know; I just can't. I think about that one time a scorpion got near our house in Quito and grandmother asked me to pick it up and throw it away and I couldn't and she called me a fag and then I cried for three hours.

There's a cart on the sidewalk. I push it next to the cat. Julio stands in the middle of the street shaking, I think. Cars start honking. Still, I cannot bring myself to pick it up. Julio can't do it either. I threaten to punch him as a driver curses out loud. Finally a short dark man comes to us from the dark sidewalk, limping. He'd been staring at us all this time.

"*Esa bestia es enorme,*" that's a huge creature, he says in his street Spanish, smiling.

Julio steps back and the man picks up the cat from its rear leg and takes a long look at it; a little blood drips from its dangling head and falls on my shoe. The man smiles in a weird way, takes the cat to the cart, drops it and limps away.

"Thanks."

The man turns around and smiles again; I hate his smile.

"It's apparent he's picked up dead animals before," Julio says.

"No shit, he's old and Salvadorian. I'm sure he's picked up dead bodies"

I push the cart over behind a huge trash container and leave it there. We hop into my Nissan and drive to Cedars-Sinai. We agree not to tell Alejandra about the cat.

The hospital room is cold, but they all are. Alejandra looks pale, but that's also normal: they've drained her blood out and given her someone else's blood. I think of how everyone should donate blood because it really saves people's lives, but do not tell Julio. What's the point? I've never donated blood. I'm kind of weird about it or maybe I'm just scared.

"How is your body reacting to the new blood?" I ask Alejandra.

"It makes me violent!" she says and laughs.

Her body is wrecked, but her spirits are better than ours.

"Oh yeah, and what does this anger make you do?" Julio asks.

"Kill small animals," she says (I swear this is true).

We laugh. I don't know how Julio feels, but I feel faintly nauseous.

"You guys look like shit," she says.

I tell Julio to tell the joke about the lady who goes over to the hospital because she's been told her husband has just had an accident.

"The wife gets to the hospital and asks the doctor how her husband is," Julio says, closely resembling a young Woody Allen.

He tries to play the characters as his joke unfolds.

"Your husband could not be better from the waist down, the doctor replies."

"How is he from the waist up? the wife nervously asks."

"Well, we're still looking for it."

There's some silence before Alejandra starts talking about her obnoxious co-workers. At some point her doctor, a blood specialist, walks in. He doesn't acknowledge Julio or myself. He talks to Alejandra about white blood cells, anemia and dieting and then walks out. Julio needs to rest because he's soon catching a plane back to Bogotá and I have to prepare stuff for my birthday party tomorrow, so we give Alejandra a hug and leave.

On the way to the car, we talk about who we'd like to be like when we "grow up."

Julio says he'd like to have a life like that of David Mamet's.

"I think Mamet wrote plays and directed his own movies, but he also did some commercial shit. I'm going to write some commercial films but using a pseudonym so that no one knows I wrote crappy shit."

Julio is surprised I don't know who David Mamet is.

I tell him I'd like to have a life like that of Andre Gide's because I love how his fiction is connected to his biography, but then I think about how, probably lured by Wilde, Gide fucked little Arab boys in Morocco and so I say I would rather live like Roberto Bolaño, the sick dog who murdered Magical Realism.

"Who?"

"He's Chilean and just died from kidney failure. He was 50. At 15, he moved to Mexico City; I think he dropped out of high school"

"I should have done that," Julio says, sounding like an old man.

"Me too. In his early 20's Bolaño moved back to Chile, a few days before Pinochet took over. Then he was jailed by the regime in Santiago, but the jailer was a childhood friend and let him run away. He went back to Mexico City for a while and then roamed about in Los Angeles, Africa, France and Spain, where he died in Catalonia as he was editing his last novel, '2666,' which is about the women of Juarez."

"*What* women?"

"Nothing. The novel's going to be something like 6,000 pages long."

"Jesus!"

We walk. The car's parked kind of far. I don't know how, but we start talking about the right way to die and we both agree that suicide is the way to go. Julio, echoing Nietzsche, says something about virtue and about having power over your own end.

"Meeting death instead of having it meet you," he says.

"Yeah, suicide is an appeal to freedom," I say.

"You're echoing the Stoics."

"Fuck yeah."

We agree that in this life, we just want to get drunk, fight, meet women and then meet more women and then write. I ask him to fight me.

"Okay, but no punching in the face," he says, taking off his glasses.

We wrestle for a while (I'm stronger). I feel the cold air on my face.

"You know man, there should be a great explosion in the sky, a solar eclipse or at least heavy rain every time someone dies, but *mierda,* nothing ever happens," he says.

We cross the street and see the great Beverly Center mall right behind us.

"That shit's not a building. It's a huge plastic pyramid," I say or he says or we both think it or something before getting in the Nissan and starting the tedious drive across Los Angeles to LAX.

2003

Peruvian *Ceviche*

I recently asked a Japanese friend, Mototsugu, about what goes into *miso soup*. He mentioned water, salt, seaweed, onions, tofu, and of course, the traditional miso paste, usually made from fermented soybeans.

"But I always taste garlic. Does miso soup have any garlic in it?" I asked offhandedly.

His eyes widened and his lips tightened. I knew I'd messed up.

"No, no, no," he said, trying to remain calm, "that's *Korean* miso soup, *doenjang*. Japanese miso soup does not contain any garlic."

I've had both the Japanese and the Korean kind and —*sumimasen*, my friend— I can't tell the difference. I do, however, understand why drawing a culinary border is so critical to national pride, particularly between two nearby countries. Once I almost walked away on a friend who claimed she had liked Ecuadorian food, but felt it was "pretty much the same" as Peruvian food. It took a lot, but I didn't walk away. I am not a culinary extremist.

But my mother is.

As an Ecuadorian-American, I'm pretty open-minded about culinary confusion. Though I get slightly, shall we say, butt-hurt whenever someone can't tell the difference between Ecuadorian and Peruvian or Colombian food. I do enjoy eating food from other Andean countries. I've even on occasion mentioned how similar two particular dishes are. Never ever, though, have I made such a brave statement in front of my mother. I might be open-minded, but a martyr, I'm not. That lady thinks there is nothing better in the whole universe than Ecuadorian food. And she's absolutely right, particularly the way grandma cooked it in the old country.

But come on! My mother won't even *try* Peruvian food! She likes Colombian food, but you'd be a fool to voice any comparative statements. She's quite sweet before her culinary wrath gets going. I think she hates the fact that food connoisseurs often call Peruvian the most delicious Latin American cuisine. She deeply believes that Ecuadorian cuisine deserves that spot. And she's absolutely right, but writing off Peruvian food altogether is too much.

So in an unprecedented act of rebellious free will, I've chosen to write about a dish both Ecuadorians and Peruvians claim to have invented and mastered. I've chosen to focus on the holy grail of coastal Andean cuisine, *ceviche de pescado* (not to be confused with Mexican *ceviche*, which is something else). I've chosen to eat it at a Peruvian restaurant. How do I explain what I'm doing here? If my lifeless body is found in some trash container with the word *traidor* carved on my chest after this is published, well, it was my own fault.

My transgression took place at Don Felix, a restaurant near Hollywood. *Ceviche de pescado* is the simplest thing in the world. The Peruvian version contains half a plate of raw tilapia or grouper fish left to cook in lime juices with salt, pepper cilantro and yellow habanero sauce (not *habañero* as I've heard a lot of people pronounce it). It is served with half of a sweet potato, which balances out the lime juice acidity. Half of a slivered red onion is placed on top. Lettuce is usually placed on the plate as garnish. The Don Felix version is quite good. At $14.50 for what is basically a glorified appetizer, it'd better be.

The sign of fresh *ceviche de pescado* is that the fish be chewy. At Don Felix it is. And the serving is generous.

You will probably need some rice or bread to further balance out the acidity (the sweet potato doesn't cut it). At Don Felix they serve you two bread rolls on the house. But it would be best if they didn't. That's the problem with this restaurant. It's uneven. While the *ceviche* was worth coming back for, the bread was dry. While the *ají* (a kind of hot salsa) was perfectly fine, they put a white plastic spoon next to it. Plastic looks trashy. They could have at least afforded a wooden one. These little details can be annoying, particularly at a place with valet parking.

But then again, it might have been an oversight. The manager wasn't there. The waiters were too busy having a lively conversation and neglected the costumers. I'm glad there's something negative besides the tasty *ceviche* (which alas is pretty similar to the Ecuadorian one) to report back home. I mean, I can't just tell my mother how good Peruvian food is. That would be cruel. As cruel as telling Mototsugu that both Japanese and Korean miso soup variations are great in their own way.

Galina on Monogamy

We were smoking outside Club Underground in Chinatown as the indie classic "Common People" by Pulp was playing in the background. Galina, a slender 25-year-old brunette from the Bay Area, had had a couple of cocktails. The topic of monogamy came up. I guess it came up because Pablo, a good friend of mine from Mexico was also in the club. Galina and Pablo used to date, but that night he was talking to a short blond inside. His hand was on her knee.

"Aren't you jealous?" I asked Galina a little heartlessly. I had had a couple of drinks too, so I was particularly inquisitive.

Galina and Pablo aren't dating anymore, but some people find it hard to witness the person they used date hooking up with somebody else. I have personally not experienced that bubbling anger since the fifth grade, when a girl I used to talk to during lunch suddenly decided talk to a taller guy in the sixth grade instead. It wasn't a good feeling and I do not intend to experience it again.

"I actually helped him talk to the blond," Galina said proudly, smiling.

She has a pretty smile and uses it a lot.

"I wouldn't be able to help an ex get with someone else," I said. "That's, like, *really* evolved."

Was I being sarcastic? I don't even know. If there was any sarcasm there, Galina didn't pick up on it.

But then again, seeing that as many as half of all married people have had a sexual encounter outside of marriage, having an open attitude might be the way to go, especially while single.

She started telling me how after breaking up with Nick, a guy she lived with for four years, and who does not talk to her anymore, she became more open.

"Knowing that people are not replaceable helps," she said.

"What do you mean?"

"If you're in a long-term relationship, you have to be flexible, so it lasts. Rigid things break, flexible things last," she said, motioning with her hands as if bending an imaginary rubber ruler.

My journalistic instincts wanted personal details —if possible, names— so I pushed a little.

"So you would let your boyfriend cheat on you..."

"It wouldn't be cheating, so long as I knew about it. Plus, it would go both ways."

"I thought only men were like that. Women are more naturally monogamous, no?"

"Women are way more sexual than men think," she said.

I couldn't push any further. Or rather, I could have but sort of chickened out at the weight of her statement. I mean, how could you follow that—"Now tell me, honey, how exactly are women more sexual than men?"

Even I have my limits. So there was some silence.

Until she spoke again.

"I'm dating this guy now —a documentary film-maker, who's in Boston promoting his new feature right now— and I don't know what he's up to. There are so many attractive people around."

I looked around. It was true.

"How can you expect somebody to not want to be with them? So long as he uses protection, I'm okay with what he does."

This was a miracle. Before me was woman who truly saw the world through male eyes. She *was* evolved! I took back my earlier sarcasm.

"How about you?" I asked her, full of admiration at this new kind of woman.

"Yes, it goes both ways. Flexibility," she said, making the rubber ruler motion again, "makes things last a long time."

At this point Pablo was making out with the blond, who was apparently from Kentucky. Galina didn't care, or pretended not to care.

"Again. It all goes back to the fact that people are not replaceable. Nobody is ever going to replace Nick," she said. "I used to be more idealistic before. Now I know that even if you meet somebody else, however cool they are, people can't replace other people. And that's a good thing!"

"But doesn't that mean you just don't care enough about the person you're dating?"

"What do you mean?"

Now it was *my* turn to speak for the entire male

gender. It was *my* turn to show her how evolved *I* was.

"If I saw an ex-girlfriend of mine with another dude, I would feel uncomfortable. If I saw a guy kissing my girl, I would punch him right away."

I could see the disappointment in her face. She took a deep breath.

"You need to learn not to care. Well, it's not that you don't care. You care, but you need to learn how to let go, like in Buddhism, you know?" Her tone was didactic.

"I guess. Maybe I'm just a conventional South American Catholic, after all."

She laughed. I laughed. It was cool.

After sobering up, I dropped Galina and Pablo off at their apartments. Since he lives close to Club Underground in Chinatown, I dropped him off first. The Kentucky blond did not go home with him.

Galina and I were quiet for a bit as I drove her to her apartment in Echo Park. She was thinking about something. Then, suddenly, she said that at one point she thought Pablo and she were falling in love, but then realized it would just be a beautiful, long-lasting friendship instead.

"You know, it's funny how people are," she said, before getting off the car. "If I hadn't seen Pablo fooling around with that blond tonight, I probably would've gone home with him. It's not that I mind he was with another girl. Like, I even helped him talk to her, you know. It's just that seeing somebody with somebody else, doesn't make you want to..."

"I get it," I said. "One girl at a time."

"Exactly. I don't really care. You have to learn how to let go. But one girl at a time, one per night," she said, laughing, "that's a good rule."

She said goodnight and walked up the long stairs to her apartment, which is nicely perched halfway up a steep hill overlooking Echo Park.

War Videogames and Heavenly Omens

I'm here at a cybercafé on 6th and Alexandria in the middle of Koreatown in Los Angeles, California. It is exactly 4:32 in the afternoon and outside the temperature is 76 degrees and the sun feels like the California sun always does. I'm the only Hispanic person in this dark, long room with PCs on both sides. The other clients are Korean teens that come here to play war video games.

The Korean owner is also around. He is 50-something and wears thick glasses. I think there's vodka in that glass he never lets go of. He charges $3 per hour for computer usage, which strikes me as too much. I just told him he should charge me $2.50, as I come here all the time, but he said no. He said he would give me 10 free minutes instead, such a nice guy that he is. Lately, I have had to pay for computer access because last summer, a man —I assume it was a man— came in through my apartment's back window and stole my Apple, just like that. He didn't take anything else. Since then I have not had a computer. It's strange, comedic really, that a guy who calls himself a writer should lack such a basic tool.

So I have an hour and 10 minutes to write. This is what I have in my head: Last Saturday —that is, two days ago— I met two friends, Pablo and Sinae, at the New Beverly Cinema. I got there early. As I was waiting in my car at the corner of Beverly and Formosa, I went through something that could be part of a Paul Auster novel.

Many Jewish men dressed in black were out that night, with their beards and their sideburns, their black hats and their suits, probably coming to or from a nearby temple. I was in my car, in my own world. I wasn't feeling well. I don't know which came first, agitation or sadness. I don't know. There was a war inside—a heavy feeling. That much I know.

At that very moment, a man wearing glasses who was walking down the street stood by my car and waved at me. I put the passenger window down, pretty bothered.

"Are you the man from the other day at the Jewish doctor's living room?" he asked.

He looked working class, whatever that means. He was trying to find something inside a white plastic bag and intently look at me at the same time.

"No. You got the wrong person," I told him.

I know I opened my big mouth too soon. I should have waited until he took out whatever he was looking for inside the plastic bag.

"Oh, I can tell it's not you," he said in a Midwestern accent, though it might have been a California countryside accent. Is there such as thing anyway?

He had a kind, plump, reddish face. I can almost say he was smiling.

"You should be glad it's not you," he went on.

"You're in better shape than the other guy. I can tell just by looking at you. Sorry"

That's all he said. He put his headphones on his ears (he carried a Discman, which now that everyone has smart phones, seems as out of fashion as going to a cybercafé). He walked away little by little, turned to the right on Beverly and kept going westward.

I was stupefied.

Who was that man who looks like me, who only a couple of days ago (I assume) was in a Jewish doctor's living room? Where did the man with the Discman meet him? How did the man with the Discman know I was feeling bad, but not as bad as the man who looks like me, my double? I don't think my sad, agitated thoughts were so obvious that somebody could see them from outside through a car window.

Whatever the case, the man with the Discman said, "You should be glad it's not you."

I couldn't help thinking about my double. Is he ill, poor, handicapped? Is he depressed?

Wait. Rewind.

The man with the Discman was going to take something out of his white plastic bag. What was it? What object did he possess that could possibly soothe my double's pain?

A few slow seconds went by.

I quickly got out of my car thinking that perhaps I could catch up with the man with the Discman, who saw that my face was the same face as my double's, the face of a pained person whom he wanted to help. I felt an instant kinship that tied me to both the man with the Discman (an unusually decent human being) and my double (a man in distress). I knew that in some way, I should, 1) Thank the man with the Discman, 2) Meet, and if possible, evaluate the Jewish doctor, and 3) Lend a hand to my double.

I hurried to the corner but the man with the Discman had vanished.

I instantly thought of Paul Auster's "City of Glass." I felt like a fictional character. I even asked myself: what if all of this was a message from God, not the soft, permissive and ambivalent South American God my elders taught me to love, but the stern Jewish God, the one I have read about in the Old Testament? This severe God could be commanding me to accept that I could be worse off, ill or deranged in a doctor's living room, getting pity from a red-faced man with a Midwestern accent.

But that line of thought is not my line of thought anymore. Many years ago I willfully chose to close off all those murky avenues from my intellectual life. I now stick to the world of man. I try, anyway.

The movie was about to start. My friends had not come yet.

I wanted to tell them what had happened. Pablo is a philosophy major at UCLA and Sinae is a freelance artist. Maybe they would understand. But show time came; I paid for my ticket, and found a seat.

Just as the movie *Army of Shadows* by Jean-Pierre Melville was starting, Pablo and Sinae showed up. It lasted over two hours. We came out after midnight. The three of us were sleepy and did not linger around after the movie. As I was driving home, I thought about creating some fiction around this event. It could be a novella where an existential detective is looking for his double, the Jewish doctor who sees patients in his living room, and the Good Samaritan with the Discman. The plot would unfold one way if the existential detective found his double and another way if he didn't. As short as the novella would be, it will probably never get written. It will stay in my head as a daydream.

**

The weekend was uneventful. I almost did not think about the event outside the movie theater. Now it's 5:15 p.m. on a Monday. I wonder what my good friend Juan David Castilla is writing right now, immersed in that traffic and cast iron noise that is New York City. I'm here, sitting at a Koreatown cybercafé in Los Angeles, California, 76 degrees outside.

I'm going to end all of this with something that comes to mind and which has no connection to the strange event at the New Beverly Cinema. Though if I were superstitious or metaphysically minded, which, as I have stated, is no longer my line of thought, or if I were a Paul Auster character, which I don't believe I am, it would certainly be related.

This happened last night. So I was sleeping in my Little Tokyo apartment. It was well into the wee hours when a stranger outside started screaming from the sidewalk outside (I live on the third floor). The screams were those of a beast in the gallows, to put it mildly. They were desperate, hurt, rabid howls that went on for hours on end. I thought about calling the police, but did not do it. I was dreaming in my bed and could half-consciously think that his vocal cords were about to shred. Those screams had such a strange impact on me that they filtered into my dreams.

I can't recall the dream's plot. Only a few images: a back alley, an old black dog, a green trash bin and a man who was screaming because somebody was not letting him in somewhere (some type of party or convention).

Who was the man screaming in my dream?

When I woke up I verified that the screams had been real. I talked to Nicky, my roomate. She said that when she was coming home really late from a party, she ran into a screaming young man who was punching the sidewalk with naked fists, crying about some love stuff. Nicky also thought about calling the police but didn't.

Again, if I were a superstitious or metaphysically-minded person, I would draw conclusions or messages based on those two weird events. But I will not. I will just let them be part of reality.

Well, the Korean owner has come up to me. He reminds me that my time at the computer is over. He stuck by his word and gave me 10 minutes of free computer usage. I look around and see that the room is still full. Not the same clients. Now there's a female, but every single one of them is playing war video games. Video games, particularly the ones about war, do not attract me in the least. My virtual wars lie elsewhere. With my stack of books, my dark skin and my three day beard I must look like an alien to these pale, beardless Korean teens with their glasses, their soft manners and their video games full of bullets and explosions. They too are like aliens to me. And yet, we exist side by side in the same cybercafé, the same 76 degrees outside, under the same sun, killing time in this long musty room in a strip mall in Los Angeles, California, in the year 2013.

P.S. From the fall of that same year: Not so good, life-changing events happened in my life later that summer (within weeks of the entry above). I should maybe reconsider my refusal to think of life in terms of destiny, heavenly omens, karma, metaphysics and stuff like that. On a lighter note, I now have a new computer!

It's Always Quiet in the End

I'm an English tutor at the Los Angeles City College and during my lunch breaks, which are supposed to last half an hour but really last an hour, I walk up to the school library, which is on the floor above my work space, and pick up random books. Most of the time I go for writers I already know, but sometimes I pick up whatever books seem interesting, usually anthologies. A few months ago, I got an anthology of modern German poetry where I found "Morphine," a poem by Heinrich Heine. The poem speaks, I think, about the pleasure of sinking into oblivion and compares death to sleep.

I checked it out and kept reading it at work because there was no one to be tutored. I read poems by Nietzsche and Hesse, but kept going back to "Morphine" because it made me think about how sometimes I turn off the light at night, close my door and window, and climb in my empty bed, not wanting anything else, not even pleasant dreams or sensations, just darkness.

**

One day Irene, the other English tutor, asks me about what I'm reading and I tell her. She's interested so I hand over the book of poems to her and ask her to read "Morphine."

There's a mirror likeness between the two
Bright, youthfully-shaped figures, though
One's paler than the other and more austere,
I might even say more perfect, more distinguished,
Than the one who'd take me confidingly in his arms
How soft then, loving, his smile, how blessed his glance!
Then it might well have been, that his wreath
Of white poppies touched my forehead, at times,
Drove the pain from my mind with its strange scent.
But all that's transient. I can only, now, be well,
When the other one, so serious and pale,
The older brother, lowers his dark torch.
Sleep is good: and Death is better, yet
Surely never to have been born is best.

Her eyes light up and I feel warm inside. Unfortunately, a tutee arrives and we work for about an hour on grammar. When I'm back, Irene is still reading the poems. She hands them over to me and asks me to let her know when I'm finished so she can go check out the book from the library. Her interest seems free from intellectual pretensions; she wants to read those poems because she was struck by what she read, that's it. Sincere reading is not far from hedonism and finding someone who understands reading that way is difficult. No, finding someone who reads is difficult. Finding someone who reads from the gut is a goddamned miracle.

Less than a month goes by, I return the book and tell Irene about it. A week later I see her walking slowly, eyes on the floor, like she does. She has the German poetry anthology in her hands. Her thick, unsteady fingers, which remind me of my grandmother's, are holding that same anthology I was holding. Her old brain, I tell myself, is thinking about the same poems I was thinking about a few days ago. I wonder. To me, Heine is part of my all-too-youthful attraction to decadence. But Irene is old and old people are not attracted to decadence. Old people are attracted to vigor. I wonder what Irene sees in those poems; I wonder what she sees in that particular poem. Could she be trying to decipher what I saw in it? Maybe, maybe not.

I look at Irene's fingers and think about Cumandá, my grandmother in Ecuador. It's not only Irene's fingers that remind me of my grandmother. There's something more to it. It isn't her personality, because Irene is rather reserved and intellectually inclined, while my grandmother is chatty and musically-inclined. It's something physical. Not her long, straight gray hair because my grandma has wavy brown hair. Not her features. Although maybe her small eyes, but not quite. Maybe her presence. Her presence and her body structure. And her honey-tinged olive skin. Irene has my grandma's glowy olive skin and walks with the same short steps. That's it. The steps.

It's been a few months since then. We never really spoke much about the poems. I think she mentioned something about "Morphine" but I can't remember. We did have some conversations, though, and not only about books. When my car broke down in the public library's parking lot, Irene offered to help me out with her AAA. She gave me her cell phone number and offered to come all the way to Sunset and Alvarado with her AAA card just so I wouldn't have to pay for a towing truck, but I was able to fix the problem and she didn't have to come. That's good, because I remember she had a migraine that day. Plus, that persistent cold she had wasn't going away. I thanked her anyway. That was very nice.

During slow work hours, we would talk and talk. I once told her about a play I had written, "The Converts," and she asked me to bring it. When I gave it to her, she did something no one else has ever done before: she sat down and quietly read my entire play in one sitting. Now that's high pain tolerance. Then we talked about the play as a whole. She was really interested. I told her about the actors and putting it on stage and what needed improvement and she said, "This is great. Reading the part about the former guerrilla fighter made me think, 'Wow, this guy really knows how to write; he even writes better than old me.'"

Maybe she was just being nice. However, the fact remains: she sat down and gave my stupid play one or two hours of her life. Again, the school library is located right above where we work. She could have read fucking Shakespeare if she had wanted to.

A couple of days later, she brought an old literary anthology where she had published a story; it was about alcoholism. She also told me about the novel she was working on and that she should work on it more. She said how when she was young she had wanted to be a nun (I told her I had also thought about being a priest when I was a kid). Then she told me how she became an alcoholic and overcame it and how it was attending Cal State LA and taking creative writing classes back in the day. We also talked about my mohawk, Thanksgiving dinners for people who don't have families, and a bunch of other stuff.

**

I didn't work during the winter. I don't know if Irene did. I think she did for a while until she was hospitalized. That cold turned out to be pneumonia and she didn't make it.

Spring semester began two weeks ago and I started working as an English tutor again. Irene used to work with mentally handicapped and autistic kids and since she is not with us anymore, I now have to work with those kids. I don't have half her tact. Plus I'm kind of lazy and she was earnest and, to be sincere, I'm scared by people with extreme disabilities. It's stupid but true. Whatever the case, I need to learn. Working with her kids makes me feel good; it reminds me of her. Last Thursday, after working with one of Irene's kids, I resumed my usual lunch trips to the library and picked up a bilingual anthology of Jorge Luis Borges' poems.

I read a poem titled "Everness." The poem begins like this:

Solo una cosa no hay y es el olvido
Dios que guarda el hierro también salva la escoria

(There's only one thing that doesn't exist: oblivion
God, who keeps iron, also saves waste matter)

Nothing really disappears. The physical world is

always changing but nothing never really ever goes away. Borges says that if God saves material things (even trash) he must also save intangible things such as thoughts, feelings and, ultimately, the soul. God's memory is all we have.

I think about Irene. She's dead. Pneumonia killed her. Her body —her atoms— will not go anywhere. But her life will, and has. I saw her in her coffin, different. Dead people become generic-looking. They retain their features and some even retain their expressions, but there's something about them that makes them look very much like one another. The body stays here. But it's just that, a body. Dead bodies have no memories, language, dreams or sentences in them. Subtle life flees. Crude matter remains.

That raving vitality we carry everywhere within and around our bodies like an electricity-charged cloud just vanishes. No one is there to incinerate our frozen dreams. It's always quiet in the end.

2006

The Brightest, Bluest Swimming Pool Water

I'm at my own
latitude / with migrant dreams—

"Dream of an Island," Shu Ting

I. Mother Tongue

Not succumbing to hyperbole when describing something you love has to be one of the toughest things in writing. So is foregoing verbal pyrotechnics to make way for terse ideas. Understated sentences that hint at underground reservoirs of feeling are harder to write than sentences bursting with obfuscating lyricism. I believe that if I had been educated in England —or at least on the American East Coast— understated writing would come more naturally to me. But the bulk of my English education took place in Los Angeles, California. I'm lucky I can sometimes write semi-coherent photography reviews.

Growing up I overdosed on poetry, too, which doesn't help.

Some of the poets that meant the most to me as I came of age were Paul Celan, Philip Larkin, Pablo Neruda, Charles Baudelaire, Stéphane Mallarmé, Jorge Luis Borges, Nicanor Parra, Charles Bukowski, Vicente Huidobro and Basho (feels weird calling him Matsuo Basho).

Of all of those poets, only Larkin truly mastered understatement; only he choose whispering over singing. Celan whispers too, but it's a more theatrical whisper, so it feels like he's not. Of all the others, even Basho likes to shock. Mallarmé is architectonic; Huidobro, painterly; Bukowski and Parra, narrative; Borges, precise but fictional; Baudelaire, musical and abstractly cinematic (anachronism, whatever); and Neruda, my first poetic father in the Harold Bloom sense, epic-minded but personal, as if Walt Whitman had been influenced by Edgar Allan Poe. Neruda's poem "Walking Around" was the single most important piece of literature in my coming of age as an artist. This very book and much of my poetry is a sort of reaction to it.

All these poets I mention are a very musical bunch. I should have read more… I don't know. See, that's the problem. I don't even know what I should have read. Emily Dickinson?

And yet, poetry is not the most influential factor on my writing. The most influential factor or force on my writing has to be Gloria Solís' Spanish. I mean just her name should tell you something. When that woman's tongue is on fire —always the case, unless she's sick or down— she can out-pace, out-maneuver and out-synonym any book-learnéd professor or coked-out car salesman out there. All she needs is her daily *cafecito* to get going. I must say my mother's use of logic is not her forte. Intensity of language is. I'm not talking about yelling or screaming (though there's plenty of that). I'm talking about a daily Spanish verbal big bang: archaisms, neologisms, guttural sounds, educated, vulgar and even made up words, all in one sentence. All words are free game when my mother feels like bombarding you with the Spanish language as it is spoken in the coastal towns of Northern South America. Grandmother was like that too.

Back when I was a kid and we still lived in Ecuador, my mother hosted three radio shows. Yes, three. She did NPR-style news, a cultural show, and a Top 40 music show. She sometimes did fictional radio stories too, in which I took part. I distantly remember sitting in the radio cabin quietly doing my fourth or fifth grade math homework while she read the news about a coup d'état somewhere far away, perhaps in the Middle East. That was how I got my pre-English language education. Out here in the U.S., my mother has for over 15 years made a living selling vitamins to other immigrants. In other words, she's still talking for a living.

I don't talk that much, but I write.

Another big influence on my writing besides the poets and my mom's verbal skills is having come to English from the outside.

As intimate as I am with English, it will never be my native language. People who know me well, can attest to the fact that whenever I'm tired, drunk or very happy —that is, when it matters— my otherwise dormant Spanish accent comes to the surface with a vengeance. To me, English has always been an outside spectacle, a foreign thing that's always one step removed. I suspect it's the same for most non-native-speaking writers.

Vladimir Nabokov's *Lolita* and Richard Rodriguez's *Days of Obligation* come to mind. The two books are vastly different. One, a classic novel about a charming pederast; the other, a beautiful non-fiction essay collection about cultural displacement. They were written over 40 years apart. And yet, their baroque prose is similar. Both have that all-out, pyrotechnic style. They play with language in a way that would seem irresponsible or pretentious in a native speaker. It's no coincidence that both Nabokov and Rodriguez learned other languages before English. They come to English from the outside. They're ESL speakers, like me.

In no way am I remotely comparing my writing style to that of a contemporary essay master like Rodriguez; or, worse yet, to that of a 20th century great like Nabokov. All I'm saying is that it looks like people who are non native speakers of a language tend to enjoy fooling around with syntax and word choice more than those who are native speakers because they can, as it were, enjoy the show from the bleachers. Native speakers, particularly those who come from countries with a long literary tradition, where all literary styles seems to have been tried before, have a more natural knack for understatement or that which is called a conversational style (think George Orwell).

As you always want what you can't have, I wish my prose was more understated and not as loud. I'm working on it. But in terms of writing even the smallest improvements take years. It took me like three years to stop writing in fragments and run-on sentences. Not long ago I thought sounding like Benjy from "The Sound and the Fury" was actually an impressive thing. Joan Didion was to blame for that phase. I'll soon find somebody else to blame, besides the poets of my youth, my mother, and the fact that I'm not a native speaker, for the current state of my English prose.

II. Gentleman Alone

He was around 40 and still living with his parents. You can hardly blame him. The villa was enormous. The house wasn't really a house. It was a mansion and he had a whole branch to himself on a different floor. Then there were the amenities: swimming pool, tennis court, jacuzzi, sauna, the garden, the piano room, the little pond with ducks, and the little chapel at the end of a slope with flowers and shrubs. How could one not live there? The parents were there to offer him guidance and company. The help was there to heat up the bread in the morning and make him natural fruit juices after he went for a swim. Lunch, he ate in the city, near the office. But at night, when he came back to the villa, if he got back home before 8:30, the security guard greeted him at the gate, and 20 minutes later, the maid brought him a plate of steak and french fries on a tray. I witnessed it many times.

It must have been a life! He could hang out with his parents in one of the six living rooms or watch the day's soccer goals on the huge television screen. When his parents went to bed, he probably stayed up for another hour before heading to his own branch; it was an apartment within a house.

It seems improbable that he brought women home. It also seems improbable that he didn't. I'm guessing he was a sexually vigorous man, who, though not particularly striking, had refined taste in his choice of suits and a funny, if self-centered, personality. There was always the apartment his mother had gifted him in the city. It was conveniently located in the same building as the office. He surely took women there. What kind of women, it's hard to tell; sometimes unwholesome women, sometimes wholesome ones. When I was a kid he introduced me to one or two of the nicer ones. They were invariably younger and blond and worked for him or were part of his professional circle. One of them stood out, Lorena. She was a nice woman who'd been his secretary. I remember her because she let me take her Nintendo home one weekend. That was a big deal for me. I wouldn't have minded her. But he wasn't the marrying type. Or he was, but only once, and for a few years at that.

Now that he's in his mid-50s, he's still unmarried, but he doesn't live in the village any longer. His parents have passed away and the village has been sold. He lives in a large apartment overlooking the city. He inherited a considerable amount of money, jewels and furniture. In the photos, I can see he kept the black piano his parents bought for the old mansion's music room and the engraved Chinese porcelain table his mother kept in the kitchen. Those two objects look out of place in his city apartment. They belong in the old mansion. I sense that he doesn't know how to live in a smaller space. Two years ago, he had somebody build him a jacuzzi in his apartment's bathroom. That also seems out of place in a city apartment. I wonder what he thinks about his own bizarre reality: being an aging, well-off, bullfight-loving bachelor in a third world country. I wonder if he even recognizes his own reality, or whether being part of it clouds his self-perception.

I have no idea.

Because, you know, *I could be wrong.* It might not be about being rich or poor, single or married, or even about living in the third or in the first world. It might be about the little things that make him an individual.

I have no idea.

The plethora of activities and little rituals that must make up this man's days and nights —now that he doesn't live in the mansion; now that he's no longer thin, vigorous, and kept— are a deep mystery to me, his only son.

III. November 10, 1995

My maternal grandparents' house. I'm alone. It's dark and pouring down as it pours down in the South American highlands. The San Pedro river is rising and the rectangular swimming pool is about to overflow and spill onto the tennis court. The little soccer field has already turned into a small pond. I won't be able to have friends over for a while. I hope the power doesn't go off. It might. Grandfather says the power outages are due to Quito's bad mayor. Grandfather knows because once upon a time he was mayor of Lago Agrio, a small city near the Amazon, which is hot and humid—nothing like cold, cathedral-laden Quito. Lago Agrio didn't even have an airport before grandfather and Texaco. He is an engineer, was in the military, helped get oil out from the jungle and for many years owned *Cine Oriente*, the biggest movie theater in the Ecuadorian Amazon. He's sick now, so the family's economy isn't what they used to be. He sold *Cine Oriente* and is now living on savings. That's a big deal for all of his nine children, six of whom are females. In South

America, if you go down from upper to middle class (or from there to working class) chances are you're never moving up ever again.

Nobody's home now. I stare out the window.

The moon is out just under the heavy clouds. It might hail. My cousins Cesar Andrés and Gabriel Leonardo make great hail men. I hope it hails. Mom will be late. She has to take care of everything before we go. I forget. We're leaving tomorrow, but maybe not. A year ago she said we'd move to Switzerland and I got all ready and we didn't end up going. In any case, I can handle moving. Life's been random so far —only child, divorced parents, five different schools, including a military academy and a Waldorf school— and I'm just in the seventh grade. I'm shrewd like a grown-up. So is mom. Dad is abroad on a business trip and we won't need his signature to get me out of the country. Some legal thing. Otherwise I wouldn't be able to go. Dad would not sign the paper in a million years. It's crazy: if we actually leave for the United States tomorrow, I won't have friends over to play soccer with next week. Not here. Maybe in the United States.

An idea: with the lights off, I won't notice if there's a blackout.

The sun is not out yet. Grandparents, aunts, cousins —all from mom's side— are at the airport. Everyone knows (there's crying and hugs). *I know.* I also know the visa thing. It's only a tourist visa, but we are moving there. It makes me nervous, but grandfather says if you tell the gringos you want to move to the States, they don't let you in. He's worked with them for Texaco; he knows. Plus, Uncle Xavier has his own business in Los Angeles. And mom's new boyfriend says the visa thing is a no-brainer.

Anyway, we hop in the plane. I'm actually thrilled about Los Angeles. I've seen "Saved by the Bell," "Mr. Belvedere," and "The Fresh Prince of Bel-Air." Plus when I was about six, grandmother had all of us (cousins, uncles and aunts) fly to Disneyworld. I still remember. I loved the United States. It was all so shiny and new. Dad will be furious though. He hates mom's new boyfriend. I heard they once ran into each other at a *cevichería* and dad slapped him in the face. That's dad's version, anyway. I don't always believe dad's version of things.

We're not telling dad and that's the end of it.

Dad's cool, like a fun uncle, and he has a sauna and a rotating bar in the middle of his pool and we go to the soccer stadium, the movies, and the mall when he's around, but mom is mom, and she sucks sometimes, but I'm choosing to go with her and her new boyfriend to the United States and this is the right thing to do, because, for instance, what if her new boyfriend turns out to be an asshole?

The plane stops in San José, Costa Rica (we drink a deep, strong coffee) then Mexico City, then a long time goes by and we're above Los Angeles: an endless carpet of lights. Uncle Xavier and his Honduran girlfriend — where *is* Honduras?— pick us up at LAX. The air in Los Angeles feels heavy. We take the U.S. Route 101 North, pass downtown and exit in Chinatown. Uncle Xavier's apartment is on the fifth floor. There's a tall black man with a gold ring in his left ear sitting in the living room. Besides soccer players in Ecuador, he is the first black man I've ever met. "No hablar Español," he says, smiling.

I don't reply. Little do I know that eventually Mike, 52, from Trinidad and Tobago, would become my first

L.A. friend and my first informal English teacher in the United States. All the adults toast and talk and then the lights go off. Everyone goes to bed: Uncle Xavier and his girlfriend in one room; mom and her boyfriend in the other room; Mike on the floor, on a mat. I sleep on a pull-out bed in front of a big window. Through the window I can see the downtown Los Angeles buildings: lights, planes, helicopters. I hear all the noise. I try to think, but the last several hours stretch abnormally long in front of me, shapeless and layered. It's too much information to take in. Mike snores like thunder! An owl is perched on a wire outside the window. I look at it for a long time. It's the first owl I've ever seen. There aren't owls in Quito. Or at least I've never seen one.

I go to school two days later. Second semester of the 8th grade. At school in Quito you wear a white shirt, a blue tie and a small golden pin right above your heart on your cardigan, and you stand in line and sing the national anthem at 7:00 a.m.. And you get up when a grown-up walks in the classroom and you take your shoes off to show your crisp white socks if asked to. In Quito, the private school buildings are white and smell like new. In Los Angeles, Highland Park to be precise, Florence Nightingale Middle School is bleak and dirty, and the buildings are square like a hospital or a prison. The kids have no manners, but they don't care and don't even know better.

And you can't wear a hat to school in Los Angeles because, you know, brown brother, the gangs.

The gangs? Really?

Most of my classmates are from Mexico and Central America and though I just got to the States, I know more English than most. In Quito, we were reading "The Iliad" and the tests were hard. In Los Angeles, we repeat words out loud, walk around, do crossword puzzles and cut out little pictures.

The months fly by. I can't graduate junior high. Bad grades. Suspensions. Those kinds of things. I get into three fights in two months. I want dad back and grandfather back and grandmother back and Cesar Andrés back and Gabriel Leonardo back and my preppy school uniform back and the hail men back and my warm swimming pool with friends over every afternoon back. Above all, I want some room. I want to walk around my property, not freeway overpasses. Instead, I get a notebook for words and a Discman for the hours. I cling to both because the hours run slow and English words pour in from all sides like the California sun.

Dad and I talk one year later. Or is it two years? He's not angry. There are tears and lots of plans when we talk, but I'm a teenager now. My head is somewhere else: legal papers, home deportations, shedding the Spanish accent, girls, punk rock, becoming a painter and reading books. A wall has been erected between Ecuador and I. It's not like I could go back even if I wanted to. Getting my legal situation fixed takes a bit longer than we all thought: twelve years, to be exact. Not a big deal. Only most of my life.

The really funny thing is, I could go back to visit the old country now if I wanted to, but I won't. Grandmother has died, Cesar Andrés and Gabriel Leonardo have gotten married, the house with the soccer field has been sold. And dad, well, dad and I, we just don't know each other that well anymore. He owns a slick fashion magazine, takes Facebook photos with models, and puts on some of the best runway shows in South America. I, on the other hand, roam the streets of L.A.

with Fante and Bukowski on my mind as if trapped in Neruda's poem, "Walking Around."

Sometimes I feel like my lungs would burst like an over-inflated balloon if I were to go back to the old country now. Like, up in the highlands I would get the worst *soroche* (altitude sickness) known to man and perish on the spot. It doesn't make sense. Like, after having flown many times, I now have a worsening flying phobia. Like, I make up excuses like being broke or not successful enough not to go back yet. Like, I can't even talk about it. Like, I've already died once and I'm not strong enough or brave enough or desperate enough to die again just yet.

IV. The Brightest, Bluest Swimming Pool Water

I'm 30 years old and drive a beat-up, light purple 1997 Toyota Corolla. Besides constant trips to Sonoma County for a girl, this little car takes me over the same Los Angeles streets day after day. On weekdays, I normally get in the car at 8:40 a.m.; roll down the windows, turn on some loud music, and rush to work. First I go west on 3rd Street for about four minutes, then south on whichever side street looks less crowded, then west on Wilshire for three minutes, and finally down a block south on Oxford. I enter a parking structure that looks like a dinosaur's rib cage and park near the stairs on the third floor. On most days I roll the windows back up, but sometimes I forget. At this point it's usually 8:56. I start work at 9:00.

Describing the landscape that surrounds you is hard because you're immersed in it. I can describe places like

Syracuse, New York, where I went to grad school; or Quito, where I spent the first twelve years of my life; or even cities I've visited as a tourist, like Santa Fe, Savannah, Toronto, and Cali (Colombia). But ask me to describe the Koreatown section of Wilshire Boulevard and I choke on all the details. Being away from a place helps you remember only the most essential details. Time and distance filter out the clutter.

But let's give it a try. Here's the Koreatown section of Wilshire Boulevard in one sentence: a broad flat stretch of cars by a mishmash of mid-sized steel and glass buildings, churches, art-deco structures and apartment complexes with smog-heavy downtown about three miles to the east and Santa Monica Beach's bright coast about fifteen miles to the west. That's a jumbled up sentence if there ever was one, but so is that Babylonian phenomenon called Wilshire Boulevard where I work. I could try to describe Echo Park, Hollywood, the 101 Freeway, downtown and other places where I usually drive around day after day, but describing Koreatown is enough. It features all I love and hate about Los Angeles.

Here's what I want to get at. A couple of days ago, I had a dream in which I was driving my Corolla to work as usual. Everything was the same as in reality, except in my dream I could see things more clearly. The bright blue sky, the noisy helicopters, the oily air, the freeways, the strip malls, and the most significant thing about L.A.'s architecture: a feeling that the city's visual core never outgrew, and will never outgrow, its pastel-colored 1970s cheap motel aesthetic. This can be seen in the scores of mid-priced motels transformed into apartment complexes that cater to immigrants and relocated Midwesterners waiting for their big break.

Whatever their price-range, most of these apartment complexes have a swimming pool in the middle, a parking lot underneath, and a gilded/refurbished overall feel. As noted in Nathaniel West's classic Los Angeles novel, "Day of the Locust," places like these flaunt their theme park architectural styles as if it were something to be proud of: Egyptian-inspired, Old-Southwest-inspired, Miami-inspired, British-inspired, Spanish-inspired, Italian-inspired.

They're soul-crushing.

Just because you sign a contract and the building now calls itself "Chateau Gardens" instead of "Hollywood Inn," it does not mean you live in an actual home. You live in a 1970s motel.

Back to my dream. I was driving to work with the windows down, when suddenly but subtly, Wilshire Boulevard morphed into *Calle Manuela Cañizares,* the stoned-paved street where I used to live in Capelo, a pastoral, high-end neighborhood outside of Quito.

Here I was, same age as now, in my beat-up Corolla, driving down a street that was both Koreatown and Capelo. The sense of unity was amazing. Instead of apartment complexes to my left and right, I saw the open grasslands of my youth. As every day on my way to work, I had the windows down, and was listening to loud music, but now the cut grass and eucalyptus smell of the old country was all around. I drove down to my grandparent's villa, which was located in a low canyon between the San Pedro river and two green slopes. This was the last place where I lived as a 12-year-old before moving to the United States with my mother and her boyfriend.

I got to the entrance. It was the same heavy black metal gate with arrow-shaped spikes on top. I opened it and parked my Corolla next to the old white house with Spanish tiles. It was about 9:00 a.m. on a weekday, but instead of jaywalking across Oxford Street and taking the elevator in the Radio Korea building, where I work as an English teacher of all of things, I walked down some stone stairs with dark green moss in their crevices. I turned left at the edge of the house and found Uncle Xavier sitting by the edge of the tennis court. He pointed to my other uncle, Daniel, who was playing soccer shirtless with two kids: Cesar Andrés and Gabriel Leonardo, my cousins, my brothers. They were playing on a green soccer field with bright white goal lines and pine trees all around. To the right was the rectangular swimming pool of my childhood. I had no time to talk. I took my shirt and shoes off (no time to take off my work pants) and plunged into the brightest, bluest swimming pool water I have ever seen.

Thank you, in no particular order:

John Matkowsky, Adrian Ravanour, Bianca Barragan, Antonina Barankevich, Mamá, Papá, Melanie and *abuelita* up in heaven, Kathy and Allan Dietkus, Pablo Velázquez, Kheskanya Sangkratok, John Jason, Patricio Donoso, Carlos Serrano, Angela Albert, Juan David Castilla, Adriana Cuestas, Paulo Yáñez, Carolina Díaz, and all the people mentioned in these essays. I would also like to particularly thank the amazing Grady Miller who revived this project when I had almost given up on it. Keep the chorus singing, my friend.

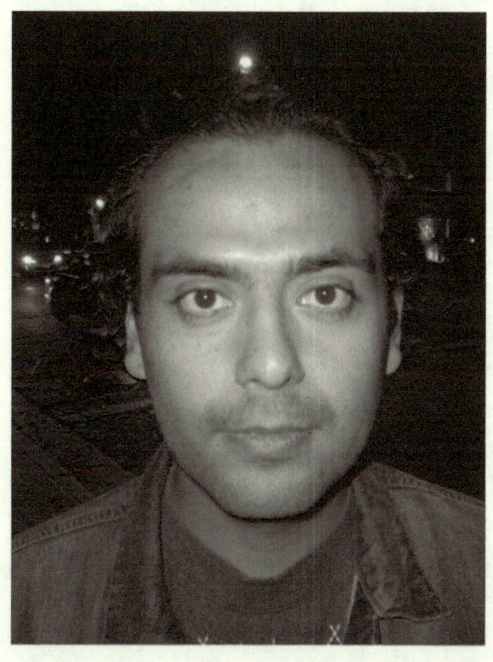

Patricio Maya Solís was born in Quito, Ecuador in 1982 and moved to California in 1995. He writes about the visual arts and politics for several print and online publications. Literary magazines *Mantis* (Stanford University) and *Verbal Seduction* (Syracuse University) have published his poetry. He holds an M.A. in Arts Journalism from the S.I. Newhouse School at Syracuse University and a B.A. in English from CSULA. In 2011, Maya was Visiting Scholar at CalArts' Politics and Aesthetics program. This is his first book of essays. He's currently writing a novel.

www.ingramcontent.com/pod-product-compliance
Lightning Source LLC
LaVergne TN
LVHW090952080826
845145LV00003B/983

* 9 7 8 0 9 8 6 2 7 3 4 0 7 *